RUGBY WORLD '99

EDITED BY

Nigel Starmer-Smith
and Ian Robertson

Queen Anne Press

A QUEEN ANNE PRESS BOOK

© Lennard Associates Limited 1998

First published in 1998 by
Queen Anne Press, a division of
Lennard Associates Limited
Mackerye End
Harpenden, Herts AL5 5DR

A catalogue entry is available from the British Library

ISBN 1 85291 591 9 (paperback)
ISBN 1 85291 590 0 (hardback)

Production Editor: Chris Marshall
Cover Design/Design Consultant: Paul Cooper
Reproduction: The Colour Edge
Printed and bound in Slovenia

The publishers would like to thank Colorsport for providing most of the
photographs for this book.

The publishers would also like to thank Allsport, Chris Thau,
Inpho/Billy Stickland, Slattery PR, SpedeGrafix and Terry Sellick for
providing additional material.

CONTENTS

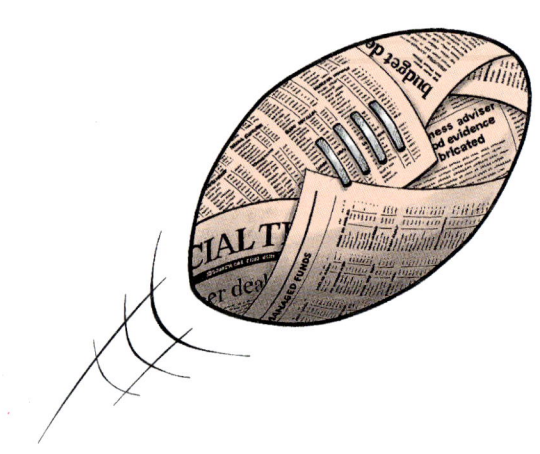

WE ALSO HAVE A PASSION FOR FOOTSIE

We know our way around the FT-SE index and the stock market like others know their way around the rugby pitch. In fact, in the investment field, few are a match for Save & Prosper.

To find out how Save & Prosper can help with your savings and investment plans, call us free on 0800 282 101.

**SAVE &
PROSPER**

UNIT TRUSTS · PEPS · PENSIONS · BANKING SERVICES

FOREWORD

BY **HRH THE PRINCESS ROYAL**

BUCKINGHAM PALACE

It gives me great pleasure to write the foreword to this book which reflects yet again the involvement of the Wooden Spoon Society with the game of Rugby.

As Patron of the Society, I am delighted to give recognition to the considerable number and variety of projects they successfully undertake each year for the benefit of many children and young people in the United Kingdom who are otherwise disadvantaged.

I was pleased to see the opening this year of the first of two Wooden Spoon Society Teenage Cancer Trust Units, one in Manchester and the other in Birmingham. I was equally delighted at the foundation of the Wooden Spoon Society Young Carers Trust administered by my own charity The Princess Royal Trust for Carers.

In the game of rugby the Wooden Spoon sponsored New Image Rugby for Players of All Abilities grows apace bringing the thrill and spills of the game to youngsters who would normally not aspire to play the game at all.

Rugby Football is a game of great commitment requiring reserves of energy, enthusiasm and skill that are translated into a physically demanding and invariably exciting spectacle.

The Members of the Wooden Spoon Society bring the same attributes to their fund-raising activities for the benefit of others.

Please enjoy this book but also support the Charity which created it and extend your enjoyment beyond these pages into the work of the Wooden Spoon Society.

Anne

Her Royal Highness opens the Wooden Spoon Society wheelchair terraces at Murrayfield, accompanied by Wooden Spoon Society President Peter Scott.

Wooden Spoon Society
- the Charity of British Rugby

Royal Patron: HRH The Princess Royal
Patrons: Rugby Football Union • Scottish Rugby Union
                     Welsh Rugby Union • Irish Rugby Football Union

When you donate to a charity, any charity, is there not a question that lurks in the back of the mind? No, it's not 'Can I have a VAT receipt?' More likely it's 'What will they do with *my* money? Will they spend *my* money wisely?' In fact 'spend' is probably not the word; rather will they *invest* it wisely? Here is a chance for Wooden Spoon to set the record straight. How much of *your* money do *we* invest in children and young people? How much does it cost *us* to do it? Fair questions. Read on.

When we set out those few years ago we really had the most modest of aspirations in garnering cash to help life's wooden-spooners. A golf day here, a dinner dance there, a few memorable stag nights at Twickenham's Rose Room – such was the extent of our fundraising. Well, things are much different now. We've grown, but the essential philosophy of Wooden Spoon has not changed. Our policy remains to raise as much money as we can, to spend as little as we need and to ensure a 'product' of high enough quality that Corporate Britain is happy to pay for it!

Glance at the names of the advertisers and contributors in this publication – magic names, generous people, Spoon supporters. Reflect on the publication itself – great articles, fascinating topics, gifted writers. In fact a perfect product. To raise money, Wooden Spoon organises events – be they golf days, dinner-dances or, as in this case, a yearbook. Make the product good enough and the public will buy and buy and buy again. Quality is not something to aspire to but rather the foundation of all things above it.

Back to the question. In our last financial year our administration cost was a fraction over 8 per cent and our promotion cost a fraction under 4 per cent. Put another way, 12 pence of every pound that we collected – as a donation, in membership dues or as the net proceeds of our 70 to 80 events each year – was spent in running the show. Eighty-eight pence went to the children and young people to whom the money was intended to go! And if we multiply that 88 pence a million times, what do you, our members, have to show for your support and generosity? Again, read on. Here are some examples of what we have done with the money in the past several months. It is by no means a comprehensive list – we have chosen those projects with a rugby interest! But if you would like a fuller picture, why not join us and be kept up to date on a regular basis?

The Wooden Spoon Society-BT Pay to Play Scheme in Scotland has now completed its second year. The scheme is dual-purpose and is strongly supported by the Scottish Rugby Union and a plethora of involved sponsors. Besides BT, who badge the scheme, the sponsors are Standard Life, Ernst & Young, Shepherd & Wedderburn, TSB Bank, Stocktrade, and Scottish Rugby, whose editor, Sean Lineen, is our squad manager, assisted by Iwan Tukalo as coach, when Jim Telfer is not around!

The scheme has two plans. First, there is the Rugby Plan, which involves and benefits affiliated rugby clubs in Scotland. Through the Rugby Plan, and with the help of the SRU's Youth Development Officers, we select, train and introduce to competitive rugby youngsters from a social environment where rugby is not the obvious game of choice. The culmination of the Rugby Plan is to send an Under 16 squad on tour to the Republic of Ireland. In the first year the scheme produced immediate success, with Ross Armour from Williamwood High School making the Scottish Under 16 Schools side. Also, Martin Yorston played a key role in helping Glasgow Under 18s win their district championship.

For the other half of the scheme, the Charity Plan, we have elected to support our Royal Patron, Her Royal Highness, The Princess Anne, and another of her charities, The Princess Royal Trust for Carers, to establish a Wooden Spoon Society Young Carers Fund. Many young people are carers – they look after disabled dads or mums or other family members, sacrificing precious childhood and opportunity in the service of others. The Wooden Spoon Society Young Carers Fund aims to recognize these young people's efforts. In the first year we launched the fund with £30,000 raised through the Wooden Spoon Society-BT Pay to Play Scheme. This year we hope to double that.

Left: We had a BT Pay to Play raffle, which benefited a lot of Scottish clubs. A new Renault Mégane was the star prize. Thank you Renault for the magnificent prize, which tempted Scott Hastings and Sean Lineen to 'cook' the result.

Above: Who says they breed 'em small in Scotland? All of these Spoon Squad 'monsters' are over 6ft 1in. New Under 16 international Ross Armour is on the left.

Left: Young carers enjoy their day out at Murrayfield, particularly the attentions of Jim Telfer and Roy Laidlaw.

L ions supremo (and now scourge of the RFU) Fran Cotton took some time off from his very active life to open the first Wooden Spoon Society Teenage Cancer Trust Unit at Christie Hospital, Manchester, built at a cost of £400,000. Later this year we will open a second Wooden Spoon Society Teenage Cancer Trust Unit at the Queen Elizabeth Hospital in Birmingham. Cancer is a most wasteful disease, but test measurements have shown that if you give youngsters a chance to fight the illness within their own peer group their chances of recovery improve by as much as 15 per cent. The teenagers of today are the players of tomorrow, so let's give them every opportunity of getting there.

Above: Fran Cotton and Denis Law open the Spoon Handles, watched by Spoon President Peter Scott and Project Director Col. Paddy Smith. Peter Smith thinks Fran needs a helping hand. Top right: Nigel Starmer-Smith cuts the first sod on the site of ACE's Wooden Spoon House. Right: Max Boyce forgot his tie, but the Spoon came to his rescue. The opening of Simpson's with (l to r) Prof Ian Laing, Scottish Chairman John Gumley, software inventor Peter Badger, Scott Hastings, Corey, and Sean Lineen Right: Rugby stars of tomorrow – with their dads – who have passed through the caring hands of Simpson's. (L to r) Scott Hastings with Corey and Kerry Anne, Sean Lineen with Cameron, and Big Gav with Robert.

Near Oxford an organisation called ACE (Aiding Communication in Education) plies its compassionate and effective trade. The ACE Centre advises on the complex needs of physically disabled children with communication difficulties, and it does so out of two portakabins borrowed from a local school. Not for much longer, though. In 1999 ACE will move into a brand new, purpose-built building, Wooden Spoon House, to become part of the National Centre for Assistive Technology.

In Scotland we totally funded and equipped an innovative Wooden Spoon Society Computer Monitoring System for the NeoNatal Intensive Care Unit at the Simpson Memorial Maternity Pavilion in Edinburgh. The system is a mind-blowing combination of software and medical good governance that allows fathers in their offices and grandparents overseas to log on to the NeoNatal Unit through the internet to get up-to-the-minute information on the young'un. It is estimated that a newborn baby is woken from its much-needed recovery sleep 36 to 40 times in every 24-hour period for checks on temperature, heart rate etc, etc. No longer at Simpson, where these measurements are now taken every few seconds throughout the day with the baby not even blinking an eye!

Across the sea in Belfast we triggered off the funding for a new nursery built at Mitchell House Special School. Not only did we trigger off funding but we managed to persuade Willie-John to part with his very precious British Lions mascot. Mind you, Willie-John has been on so many Lions tours he probably has an entire pride of Lions back there in Ballymena!

In the Home Counties we had two more magical moments in 1998. First, Jeff Probyn did the honours by opening our Wooden Spoon Society Adventure Playground at the Whitefields Centre in Walthamstow, East London. This quite extraordinary school for children with special needs is divided into six school houses, each catering and caring for a particular need. One such house caters for children who are born both blind and deaf.

Can there be a greater handicap and can there be a better Wooden Spoon cause than the Whitefields Centre? Sadly, yes; there are many, and members of Wooden Spoon do what they can to fulfil their needs. Again in the Home Counties we created the Wooden Spoon Society Occupational Therapy Gymnasium for brain-damaged children, as part of the redevelopment of Tadworth Children's Trust at Tadworth, Surrey.

Above: Big Willie John does the honours at Mitchell House.
Left: Jeff Probyn cuts the tape to let play begin at the Whitefields Centre, Walthamstow, East London.
Below: Tim Rodber, appropriately kitted out in his Spoon colours, helped us withour Tadworth Court project.

In the Principality, meanwhile, we opened a splendid hydrotherapy pool at the Caerphilly Children's Centre, which is a boon to all the children with special needs, who now get so much benefit from the healing properties of water.

The above are only a selection of the many projects that Wooden Spoon Society undertook to fund and complete over the past several months. Our policy of Local Funds for Local Projects means that each of our regions not only raises funds locally but keeps them in and for that locality. Central resource then adds to the money raised, on a pound- for-pound basis, to enhance the total contribution.

By joining Wooden Spoon Society and working with our regional committees you can do your part to help the special needs of children in your community. That must be worth the effort of joining, belonging to and being part of your Wooden Spoon Society. We need a lot more 88 pences so that we can reduce our 12-pence costs to just 6 pence. Complicated? Difficult to understand? Ring the Spoon Office if you want an explanation of how simple it is to do.

For details of membership of Wooden Spoon Society, ring, fax, email or write to:

The Spoon Office, 35 Maugham Court,
Whitstable, Kent CT5 4RR.
01227 772295 (tel); 01227 772296 (fax)
Email:charity@woodenspoonsoc.org.uk
Website: http://www.woodenspoonsoc.org.uk

REACH FOR THE BEST

It's rare to find a recruitment consultancy who tackle personnel requirements with such tenacity and unfailing dedication. An unrivalled approach that has enabled Pertemps to remain unchallenged at the top of the league as the UK's leading independent recruitment consultancy.

As market leaders, we have developed our reputation not just by "filling positions" but by adding value to our client portfolio, a philosophy which is reflected in the diverse range of leading blue-chip companies that currently utilise our services.

Operating in three service divisions: commercial and professional, industrial and driving and technical and executive, our fully integrated service ensures that we are able to deliver quality personnel with the right skills, in the right place at the right time.

So, if you are seeking to win the competition for business, make sure that you retain the competition for talent by choosing Pertemps, Britain's most successful independent recruitment consultancy.

PERTEMPS
recruitment partnership
....

Head Office: Meriden Hall, Main Road, Meriden, Warwickshire CV7 7PT.
Tel: 01676 525000 Fax: 01676 525009

RUGBY WORLDWIDE

PROFILE OF CHRISTIAN CULLEN

BY **RAECHELLE EDWARDS**

Local hero, national hero – Christian Cullen's footballing skills and electric pace have catapulted him to the top of the Rugby Union tree.

Word has it that Christian Cullen is so integral to life in his home town, Paekakariki, that his dashing try-scoring feats have prompted the local pubs, showing the rugby Tests live on the big screen, to offer to serve free beers to the regulars from the time the young All Black sensation first touches the ball until the moment that he posts his first five-pointer. Naturally the drinkers aren't happy, because the dynamic full back's habit of crossing the try line at lightning speed means that they can't take advantage of the gimmick.

Cullen's prolific scoring rate was on show from day one. On international debut against Western Samoa in 1996 he ran in a hat-trick of tries. Then in his second Test against Scotland in Dunedin – which New Zealand's coach John Hart rates as his best all round game to date – he came away with four. And one in the first half was truly unbelievable. With the ease of a cat slinking through a narrow gap in an open doorway, gracefully and not even touching the sides, he beat seven tacklers, both physically and with his step, to glide straight through and score under the posts.

Cullen's confident risk-taking and downright guts have been glimpsed on numerous occasions since his marked arrival into the senior All Black side.

'It was a pretty good start getting three tries in my first Test and four in the second. In my third I was brought down to earth pretty quickly when I had a shocking game in Eden Park against Scotland. Yeah, it was just one of those starts, I suppose. I got put over for a few easy tries. I just fell over the line,' Cullen shrugged.

His words are refreshingly modest. Maybe that is because his deeds on the football field clearly illustrate his ability to devastate, so like a true champion, he doesn't need to tell anyone how good he is.

Many teams from around the globe have been exposed to his unpredictable and exciting impact play. Last year in the Bledisloe Cup match between New Zealand and Australia in Dunedin, Cullen took a wide pass and easily outmanoeuvred the Wallabies' defence. The series of events involved Stephen Larkham catching a bomb at full back, putting up a high kick and chasing it through. The All Black scrum half, Justin Marshall, took the ball and passed it out to Cullen who was in space. The wizard with the shaved head got through the first line of defence, stepped around George Gregan, then his blinding pace allowed him to outrun Jason Little, who tackled him just over the try line. It was a blistering, 70-metre effort.

The importance of his ability to seek out gaps has not been lost on retired New Zealand captain Sean Fitzpatrick. The world's most-capped forward, having played 92 Tests in total, Fitzpatrick rates Cullen as the best All Black full back he ever played with.

'I've played with some pretty good ones, but Christian really is a game-breaker…and he's got a real arrogance about the way he plays the game, which is really essential,' praised Fitzpatrick, who can relate to his style. 'He is a young guy who plays rugby with a huge amount of maturity, but he's also got that bit of daredevil, too, where he backs himself to the hilt. What he's got is a skill that no one can really learn. He turns a situation that looks like nothing is going to happen into a try-scoring opportunity, which is completely brilliant,' said Fitzpatrick with genuine admiration. And perhaps his most spectacular try is the perfect example of the trait that Fitzpatrick describes.

Cullen burst onto the worldwide scene with a try in the 1996 Hong Kong Sevens that can only really be described as freakish.

'The most amazing try I have seen him score was the one in the 7s against Fiji from behind his goal line. I was watching it on TV, and it was the last minute of the game and the All Blacks desperately needed to score a try to win. They were camped inside their dead-ball area, and Christian suddenly broke out from nowhere and there were three Fijians on him, but he slipped through and ran the length of the field,' recalled Fitzpatrick, his voice filled with the energy of an overenthusiastic commentator calling his final game. And I thought it was amazing. No other player in the world could do that. It was impossible. I just don't know how he did it,' he added in awe.

That dazzling solo try threw him into the spotlight. Spectacular performances were the norm for Cullen in the 7s competition in Hong Kong that year. He scored 18 tries in total, including seven in one match, to be deservedly crowned Player of the Tournament.

Now you see me, now you don't – Cullen at the 1996 Hong Kong 7s. His 18 tries in the competition earned him the Player of the Tournament award and announced him to the rugby world.

With Cullen having had so many highlights in his career already, it's hard to believe that John Hart is firmly convinced that he is still far from reaching the best use of his talent.

'I think he has still got a long way to go to reach his potential, which is unlimited. Hopefully he'll reach that potential some time in the next two years,' Hart speculated. I think his game has grown far beyond his performance against Scotland in 1996 – which is hard to beat – because he is now an excellent defensive player as well as an attacker. I think in the early days the emphasis was on his attack, and his defence was a little culpable. I think he has much more maturity in his all round game now,' explained Hart. He's one of those players who has the 'X' factor.'

With such unique talent, it is hardly surprising that he is the local hero in his quaint home town, which lies among rolling green hills outside Wellington. The eyes of Craig, who owns the Paekakariki Hotel, light up at the mere mention of Christian's name, which is easy to understand when you discover that his pub masquerades as a shrine, a house of rugby worship, with photographs of Cullen right from when he was born and his No. 15 jerseys framed and plastered all over the walls, so much so that young Christian is almost too embarrassed to grace the place with his presence.

'We get the crowds in for the big games, and whenever he does something good, which is pretty often, the roof comes off the pub,' said Craig enthusiastically. 'His nickname is

Cullen signs autographs for young fans. How many of these dream of being the next Christian Cullen?

"Kinny", so everyone shouts out "Go Kinny!" He's pretty humble, so he doesn't come in much now with all the memorabilia on the walls.'

Cullen's uncomplicated and earthy attitude may have something to do with his family. Christian, named after his father, began playing rugby with his elder brother in the back yard. It seems that his parents will always be on stand-by if he ever needs pulling down a peg or two.

'It's good to see Mum and Dad at the games supporting. They enjoy it and you don't want to let them down, as well as the team...so you go out there and play for your family too,' said Christian in his characteristically shy manner.

A rugby player with exceptional imagination, perception and the ability to step off both feet while running flat out, Cullen almost seems like he's checking to see whether or not he's in a dream when he talks with genuine amazement about his involvement in touring all over the world with the famous and dominant All Black team. But a life that can sometimes feel

surreal takes a sudden reality check when he remembers the sacrifices. Cullen insists that professionalism leaves little time for the New Zealanders to party seriously and create the same havoc off the paddock that they do on it.

'We have a few quiet beers after the game, but we've always got to travel the next day and we get up pretty early, so it's no fun travelling with a hangover,' he said. 'We play cards, we read a lot – sports magazines, not books – we go to the movies and we do a lot of sleeping, too, because we really need our rest.'

Cullen named winger Glen Osborne as his pick of roommates on a tour because 'he's always good for a laugh and he does stupid things sometimes which lightens things up'.

His nomination for worst person to share a room with? 'I'd have to say the snorers...there is one in the forwards and another in the backs who snore quite loudly.'

In typical tightknit Kiwi fashion he refused to reveal their identities. One feels that from the point a player enters the revered All Black fraternity, he is bound by the strongest of oaths to his fellow team-mates.

If you glimpse the determination in Cullen's eyes, it is clear that he really hates to lose. When you play for the nation that wears the black jumper, that's the best way to be because you're pretty much assured that you won't have to deal with second place. And certainly not if the man lurking at the back of the field can help it. In fact, Cullen has had the bitter taste of defeat only once in an international: on 31 August 1996, when the

On duty for Wellington Hurricanes in the Super-12. Although not a particularly heavy player in rugby terms, Cullen has deceptive strength and is hard to bring down – once, of course, you have caught him.

Cullen tries to elude the Springbok defence during the 3rd Test at Johannesburg in August 1996. The All Blacks went down 32-22, the young full back's first taste of international defeat.

All Blacks went down 32-22 to South Africa at Ellis Park in Johannesburg. That was enough to convince Cullen that he doesn't want it to happen again.

The main rugby goal Cullen makes clear he wants to achieve is holding up the Webb Ellis Trophy. There was no hesitation in his voice when he said plain and straight, 'I want to win a World Cup. Nothing gets better than the World Cup and that's one of the things I've always wanted to do.' Cardiff next year will be Cullen's first shot at achieving his aim. 'I hope we can win it. That's certainly what everyone wants to do and it's going to be tough, but I'm sure we'll give it a good crack,' he said mischievously.

Cullen will be used as an attacking weapon by the All Blacks, who will exploit the success of the angles he runs. However, unravelling the mysteries of the Cullen phenomenon is difficult even for those closest to him, so John Hart needs to give him tremendous licence. An unorthodox footballer, Cullen tends to 'wander' on the field, but his positional play is nothing short of astonishing. He is unusual in that he is so difficult to read. He surprises like a predator in the dark; his prey is rarely prepared for the direction from which he will swoop.

His genius-like creativity means that it is very difficult to plan a way to suppress Cullen for the reason that no one (possibly not even Cullen) knows when and where he's coming from. It's simply instinctive, so singling him out is a recipe for disaster. The only hope of harnessing him is to devise a strategy in which your defensive pattern covers all angles. Nick Farr-Jones once said about the great David Campese, 'He's the sort of player whose brain doesn't always know where his legs are carrying him.' That concise description also aptly sums up Mr Cullen.

Even if you catch him, Cullen is very difficult to contain. Many a player the world over has thought he has had the All Black full back in his arms, but, before he even realises it,

Cullen has managed to break free and sprint off into the distance. He is not a particularly heavy player in rugby terms, but he is very hard to tackle because he has deceptive strength. Cullen copes with weights of 145kg (320lbs) on his regular outings to the gym and is the second strongest player in the All Blacks – no mean feat for a young man who weighs only 85kg (13st 5lbs) and stands at a height of 180cm (6ft). With his attacking prowess, containing Cullen is an exhausting thought, and an opposing full back must know fear when he is hit with the shocking realisation that as the last line of defence, it is all up to him – Cullen must be stopped! It takes tough, uncompromising commitment to cut him down. If the All Black outfit is looked at as a rose bush, Cullen is not the most obvious thorn, but the one that is bound to draw the most blood. Just when you think you've escaped an encounter unscathed, it pricks you and opens a deep wound.

It is obvious why Cullen has been accorded demigod status at home. In the rugby-mad nation, he is renowned as one of the greatest rugby players ever to have graced the game. At 22 years of age he had the unparalleled strike rate of 21 tries in 22 Tests. In 1997 he equalled the world record of 12 Test match tries in a calendar year. So it would be fair to say that he probably wouldn't want to be anyone else. But if he did, understandably he wouldn't be averse to being among the elite in another sport.

'I wouldn't mind being a professional golfer and playing on all of the top courses in the world and win a few tournaments and make a bit of money – that would be great. I'd like to be Ernie Els and drive like Tiger Woods,' Cullen declared. 'I'd like to see what makes Michael Jordan tick and why he's been the best for so long. It would be amazing to find out those things.'

Here's a free tip, Christian. It's the same spirited drive and burning desire that guarantees that even if there isn't a try to be scored, you will arrive as an explosive shock to menacingly touch down from nowhere. You share his innate skill, vision and that magical sixth sense.

Which other rugby player would Cullen be if he couldn't be himself? Surprise, surprise, his choices are all Kiwis. 'It would be nice to be as big as Jonah,' he laughed. 'I guess when I was young I looked up to All Blacks like Joe Stanley, Sean Fitzpatrick and Zinzan Brooke, and I always wanted to be like them.'

One thing is for sure: if Cullen can maintain his stunning form, his name too will be featured in New Zealand's history books. Youngsters aspiring one day to don the black jersey already dream at night about becoming 'the next Christian Cullen'. And a concept that sits comfortably with rugby observers is that he's still got plenty of time and plenty of points to prove. However, as Cullen cruises along looking to realise his ambitions, it is relieving for the united rugby nations outside New Zealand to know that with the accelerated intensity of rugby in the professional era he is convinced that his life span at the top level won't be too long. 'They say rugby players' careers are getting shorter. There probably won't be many Frank Bunces who are still playing at 36. I'm hoping to be around until 28 or 29, another 6 or 7 years,' he said.

For now, though, on the field, Cullen's brilliance is hair-raising, and when it comes to putting in his all while wearing his sacred All Black jumper, never expect him to surrender. Never. For Christian, actions speak louder than words, but in his home town the tongues are wagging – Paekakariki's population are almost as fast to boast about their favourite son as he is at scoring tries. And although the local patrons have to fork out their own money to sink a few beers during an international, they wouldn't have it any other way and they will keep returning to witness the young flier's cheekiness on the park. Fierce loyalty prevails: Christian is one of their own and of that they are proud.

CATHAY PACIFIC

CONNECTIONS.

SUPER-12 '98

BY **RAECHELLE EDWARDS**

Auckland skipper Michael Jones (left) and prop Olo Brown stare defeat in the face in the Super-12 final after Canterbury ex-Aucklander James Kerr's late try.

D-day for the southern hemisphere's Super-12 rugby competition. Familiar territory, Eden Park. Provincial powerhouses Auckland were facing gutsy underdogs Canterbury. Both sides were hungry for success in the all-New Zealand affair. It was shaping up as a spiteful clash between the traditional rivals of the North and South Islands: the Auckland Blues, perceived as the arrogant and patronising big shots, and the Canterbury Crusaders, seen as the poor, down-and-out country bumpkins, better left out of the spotlight. Ultimately it was a team of stars versus a star team.

The final didn't let anyone down. It was high-impact rugby at a super-fast tempo; a tight and intense encounter with a long-standing 13-all deadlock. Irony in the end, as ex-Aucklander James Kerr scored the winning try for Canterbury. Since the Super-12 began in 1996, the Blues had never been beaten at home, and one of their own had turned the tables in the dying stages. The final score was 20-13 in the Crusaders' favour.

Although the Blues had been led gallantly by Michael Jones, who filled the void left by the loss of Sean Fitzpatrick and Zinzan Brooke admirably, Auckland were really just plain lucky to make the final. They had a controversial play-off against the Otago Highlanders.

The supporters of Otago could be forgiven for offering the referee and his assistant postmatch eye tests. This clash brought new meaning to the angry questioning shout from the grandstand, 'Are you blind, ref?' The Blues' Adrian Cashmore clinched the win with a try that should never have been given. The Highlanders' full back was taken out without the ball. Cashmore scooped it up and strolled to the line. Auckland secured their place in the top two spots for the third year running. The scoreline was 37-31.

Full credit to the Highlanders, who were the surprise package of the 1998 Super-12. There wasn't much pressure on the team, having finished last in 1997, and these low expectations meant that they flourished. The strong men up front plus the class and immense skills of Jeff Wilson out wide, all under the strong leadership of the tenacious loose forward Taine Randell, who was to become the next All Black captain, made the Highlanders a force to be reckoned with.

One South African team got a look in to the semi-finals: the Coastal Sharks, who travelled to Lancaster Park in Christchurch. The Sharks, made up mostly of Natal players, were again the most complete of the sides from the Republic. One of their strongest points was their courage and professionalism. This was demonstrated when mix-ups caused the squad to be split into four separate groups, en route to Australia and New Zealand, each taking various flights and directions to finally come together in Canberra the day before they were to meet the 1997 grand finalists, the ACT Brumbies. After such amazing circumstances, they played with great panache to win the game.

The Sharks, who brought dazzling winger Stefan Terblanche to the world stage, were the only South African team to win in Australia and New Zealand, so they deserved their date with Canterbury in the semi. The game matched the first decider in its fiery nature, in particular where the whistle-blowers were concerned. Ian McIntosh, who coaches the Sharks, was clearly unhappy with the refereeing and numerous decisions on the field. His blood was boiling as he leapt to his feet and charged from his seat to the sideline, unleashing expletives that encapsulated his frustration. Canterbury won the clash 36-32.

New All Black captain Taine Randell on the move for the Otago Highlanders. Randell and his pack plus Jeff Wilson outside made the Highlanders a force to be reckoned with. In 1998 they made the semis after a last-place finish in 1997.

The giant replica of a knight on horseback that overshadowed the ground was a charming metaphor for the fight the Crusaders put up all year on their home turf. They were a group of battlers, a fairy tale, a side with very few high-profile players – but they were a true team in every sense of the word. Canterbury lost some footing when their talented scrum half Justin Marshall snapped his Achilles tendon in the second round of the competition, but they rallied. Andrew Mehrtens began to blossom at fly half and by the end of the series he had deservedly made the All Black No. 10 jersey his own.

Of the remaining Kiwi sides, The Chiefs were in the hunt, racing for a place in the top four. However, the killer for them was that their form throughout the season was too erratic. They started with flying colours, pipping the team who were to become the Premiers by two points in their opening game. They followed this up with a successful road trip to South Africa, but then they lost to fellow New Zealand sides Wellington, Auckland and Otago in successive weeks. Being beaten by New South Wales in the final round killed off their chances of charging home to a semi-finals berth.

The other New Zealand outfit, the Wellington Hurricanes, were the most unusual. They had an awesome start, convincingly beating the Western Stormers and Northern Bulls in South Africa and defeating The Chiefs at Hamilton. To win matches away from your home ground consistently in this tournament is quite a feat, and with

An open-side flanker with pace to burn: the Western Stormers' Bobby Skinstad finds himself in space. Sadly he broke his ankle in round seven and took no further part in the competition.

quality players like Christian Cullen and Tana Umaga on hand, the future was looking bright. The turning point for Wellington was in round four, in what was arguably the most exciting of all the 69 matches. It was their first home game and they lined up against the Queensland Reds. The game seesawed for the full 80 minutes, but the Reds were triumphant at the final whistle. So began the Hurricanes demise, and from that day they lacked urgency.

In comparison it was an experimental year for South Africa, where the system of amalgamated provinces was put to the test. The Africans did not get the final results they desired, with the Sharks the only team to make the cut, but then the season had been dedicated to adjustment.

Three teams from the Republic never looked like making the final four: the Northern Bulls, the Western Stormers and the Golden Cats. The Northern Bulls managed only three wins, all of them on familiar territory at home. While they enjoyed some comprehensive victories, overall they tended to lack imagination, and they were left with no silverware. However, the Bulls have (that dirty word) potential, and if they take the lessons learned into 1999 they are likely to improve. The shining aspect of their play was undoubtedly defence, which was uncompromising. This side knew how to tackle.

Going into the season, much was expected of the Western Stormers because of Western Province's status as reigning Currie Cup champions. In the end the Stormers simply found the step up in class much more difficult to achieve than they had anticipated. The lowest point came in the ninth round, when they were thumped 74-28 by Auckland. The Stormers did, however, provide a surprise highlight for the international arena by discovering Bobby Skinstad, who is the very model of the open-side flanker of the modern era, with pace to burn. However, when he broke his ankle in round seven and failed to take any further part in the series, his side lost five in a row.

The Golden Cats doesn't sound like the name for a world-beating rugby team, and the side didn't play like one either. They won their first and last matches of the season and none in between. The only teams they overpowered were their fellow South African bottom-level finishers. The Cats were the perfect example of the troubles involved with compiling teams. Their poor showing raised questions, such as the practicality of training in Free State one day and Transvaal the next, as well as general curiosity over how a side thrown together can develop a true team spirit.

The Australian teams completely missed out. The Queensland Reds were the wounded animal in 1997, who developed into a dangerous beast not to be underestimated in 1998.

Being without speedster Ben Tune for several weeks (the try-scoring machine was nursing a broken jaw) did not help their quest for honours, but with players like John Eales roaming around the paddock it was not surprising that they still put up a good show. They needed a win and four tries for a bonus point in their last encounter to snatch a place in the semi-finals, but a loss to ACT robbed them of all hope.

The New South Wales Waratahs were a somewhat schizophrenic outfit. At the Sydney Football Stadium they were blinding – it was there that they made a meal of the Coastal Sharks, thrashing them 51-18 – but mental focus seemed to desert many of the players as they walked out through the departure gates at Sydney's international airport. It took until the very last round for the Waratahs to display their winning determination away from home as they defeated The Chiefs at Albany. The year was a great learning curve for the numerous youthful students in whom the management had put their faith. These up-and-comers gained valuable experience, and in 1999 they should be able to transfer their home success overseas. Another plus was the signing of former Springbok skipper Tiaan Strauss, who proved to be a major asset.

After the excitement of the ACT Brumbies making the final in 1997, high hopes and optimism surrounded them again. Plainly new coach Eddie Jones is not Rod Macqueen, but to be fair, injuries were particularly unkind to the Canberra-based lads. World-class players such as winger Joe Roff, scrum half George Gregan and captain Brett Robinson missed the bulk of the series and it hurt the Brumbies. On the bright side, Stephen Larkham was outstanding. He carried his team and saved it from embarrassment on numerous occasions.

What was clear again in 1997 was that one of the most incredible aspects of the Super-12 series is that you can throw away all your form guides: any team is capable of beating any other team on the day in this competition. The adjective 'super' is so appropriate. You only have to enquire why individual spectators come to watch the matches and inevitably their answer revolves around anticipation. It's like an addiction. They simply cannot wait for the guaranteed sensational spectacle they are about to be privileged to witness.

Queensland's hard-running Australian Test centre Daniel Herbert is brought to a halt. The Australian sides had a disappointing Super-12. Last year the ACT Brumbies made the final. This year none of the three sides made the play-offs.

Canterbury Crusaders' skipper Todd Blackadder holds high the Super-12 trophy after his side's 20-13 victory over Auckland, in Auckland.

THE WOMEN'S WORLD CUP

BY **ALASTAIR HIGNELL**

'Gal Blacks' right wing Vanessa Cootes races away to score one of her five World Cup final tries against the United States.

Following England's 76-0 humiliation in Brisbane, several Australian newspapers carried the story that the switchboard at the New Zealand Rugby Union (NZRFU) was jammed with demands for Clive Woodward's men to be given a fixture against the 'Gal Blacks'. That such a rumour was thought worth reporting is partly a reflection of the Australian sense of humour, partly an indictment of England's sorry performance and wholly a tribute to the new women's world champions.

New Zealand's dominance of the third Women's Rugby World Cup – the first to be fully sanctioned and, to the tune of £500,000, funded by the International Rugby Board – was even more complete than the All Blacks' dominance of the men's game. The statistics tell the brutal truth: played 5, won 5; points for 344, points against 26; tries for 56, tries against 3. From their first game, when they ran in 134 points against Germany, to their semi-final and final victories over the two previous world champions, England and the United States, New Zealand were awesome. It is now seven years since they last lost, to the Americans in the 1991 semi-finals. That, in fact, is the only match that anyone can remember any New Zealand women's team ever losing. On the evidence on offer in Amsterdam it will be a very long time before they taste defeat again.

It wasn't until their third match, at Dutch rugby's new headquarters on the outskirts of Amsterdam, that the Gal Blacks conceded their first points: a penalty kicked by Spain. It wasn't until the end of their fourth – after five hours of World Cup rugby – that they conceded their first try. England, their opponents in that match, also had the cheek to take the lead, through two early penalties from No. 8 Claire Frost. In between, they were, like all New Zealand's other opponents, simply brushed aside.

England conceded 44 points, as did the United States in the final. By scoring one more point and one more try than England could manage against New Zealand, the Americans just about justified their second place. Behind England, however, there was a huge gulf in class. After going down 72-6 to England in a pool match, Canada conceded another 80 points in the play-off for third place. Scotland fancied their chances after a Five Nations Grand Slam. However, they paid the penalty for fielding a weakened side against New Zealand after their first choices failed to gel against the United States, and then they disappointed against Australia to end up in sixth spot.

Spain were the most popular team in the tournament. Seemingly much smaller than their opponents, they battled bravely against both New Zealand and the United States before losing a pulsating plate semi-final against Australia. Victory over France on finals day meant a thoroughly deserved seventh place. The success of the Spanish team and that of Kazakhstan, who beat Wales and Ireland (twice) to take the bowl trophy and ninth place, were proof positive that rugby is continuing to make great strides towards becoming a truly worldwide game – a goal the World Cup was set up to achieve. The decision to hold the tournament in Amsterdam with the Dutch Rugby Board as efficient and genial hosts and with the backing and blessing of the International Rugby Board, several of whose delegates attended the final week, was clearly taken with the same aim in mind.

New Zealand centre and goal-kicker Annaleah Rush lines up a penalty in the World Cup final against the United States.

In the Gal Blacks, women's rugby has the perfect standard-bearers. In the past the women's game has been regarded as a bit of a curiosity, a pale and not very exciting imitation of the real thing. Whatever the truth of the matter, the majority of players had seemed neither very skilful nor very fit. This New Zealand side has exploded that myth. In Amsterdam they played rugby as it is meant to be played, with power, pace, skill, vision and teamwork.

Of course there were stars. Right wing Vanessa Cootes scored five tries in the final to take her to 35 from just 9 Tests. Left wing Louisa Wall – a netball international – was every bit as direct, while centre and goal-kicker Annaleah Rush had just the right combination of finesse and power, and outside half Anna Richards was tirelessly creative. Up front, fiery hooker and captain Farah Palmer led by example, and

Scotland full back Alison McGrandles kicks during the clash with Australia.

England's Paula George beats Canada's Sherri Sparling on her way to the line in the third-place play-off.

back-rowers Melodie Robinson and Rochelle Martin could have come off any All Black production line.

Just as importantly, and even less surprisingly, New Zealand are setting the pace off the field as well. Since 1992, when the NZRFU officially recognised the 'Gal Blacks', the links between the two have grown progressively tighter. In 1996 Rob Fisher, the then chairman, made the decision to throw the full might of the union behind the women's team. In the lead-up to the World Cup the NZRFU not only bankrolled the team, but provided everything from dietary advice to training camps to motivation – John Hart's address on the meaning of the black shirt with the silver fern was, say the team, inspirational.

As a result, rugby has been able to attract some of the best female athletes in the country and considerable interest from the media. Before they left for the tournament the team appeared on primetime television, while a marketing campaign featuring them as 'dangerously beautiful' sharks made the front page. During the tournament they received thousands of faxes from well-wishers back home. With the final shown live on New Zealand television, they were guaranteed a heroine's welcome on their return.

Once again, it's up to the rest of the rugby world to pick up a gauntlet thrown down by New Zealand. The Gal Blacks have shown what the sport has to offer to any would-be female athlete, and they've shown their rivals what can be achieved. There is a danger that other nations might conclude, as Scotland did in the tournament, that New Zealand are unbeatable, but that would be wrong, and damaging for the game as a whole. It is true that the Gal Blacks have set new standards, but they have also shown how to achieve those standards. Over the next four years their rivals will have to play a different brand of 'catch-up' rugby. New Zealand are undisputed, and deserving, world champions.

WORLD CUP RECOLLECTIONS

FARAH PALMER TALKS TO IAN ROBERTSON

On 16 May 1998, 25-year-old Farah Palmer celebrated the best moment of her rugby career when she captained New Zealand to victory in the final of the 3rd Women's World Cup. She had led her team to big wins in the pool matches; New Zealand followed up a record 134-3 victory against Germany with a 76-0 triumph against Scotland. It had been much harder in the knockout stages, but New Zealand beat Spain 46-3 in the quarter-finals, England 44-11 in the semi-finals and the United States 44-12 in the final.

A postgraduate research student at the University of Otago in Dunedin, Farah has been the first choice New Zealand hooker since 1996, when she won her first cap against Australia. At 5ft 4$^{1}/_{2}$ ins and 11 stones, she is mobile, skilful, extremely competitive and an inspirational captain. Here she looks back on two exciting weeks with New Zealand in Amsterdam.

What was the New Zealand build-up to the World Cup in Amsterdam?
'The biggest single problem for the New Zealand team is our ongoing lack of opportunity to play international matches. In 1995 we only played one match, against our traditional rivals, Australia. Fortunately with the World Cup in mind, we were able to play Australia as usual in 1996 and also we were able to organise our participation in Edmonton as one of the teams in the Canada Cup alongside Canada, America and France.

New Zealand skipper Farah Palmer hoists the World Cup after the Gal Blacks' final victory over the United States.

We had never played against these sides in my time with the team and it was an invaluable experience. We beat the host nation 88-0, America 85-8 and France 109-0. In 1997 we only had two matches, but we recorded good wins against Australia [40-0] and England in Christchurch [67-0]. As England were the current world champions this was a very significant result, which gave us great encouragement and confidence for 1998.'

Why did New Zealand not take part in the 1994 World Cup?
'Women's rugby in New Zealand was still trying to establish itself in the early 1990s, and the New Zealand Rugby Union decided that as the 1994 World Cup was unofficial and not under the auspices of the International Rugby Board they would not allow us to participate. However, in the last four seasons we have received tremendous support from the New Zealand Rugby Union and also from all the main provincial unions. It was through their financial support that we were able to prepare properly for the World Cup in Amsterdam.

'In November 1997 we named a squad of 54 players to undertake a fitness programme for six months, with all the players being tested every month. We met

Farah Palmer packs down at hooker against the United States flanked by Tracey Watecs and Regina Sheck.

regularly in groups in the Auckland area, in the Wellington area and in Canterbury and Otago. The final squad was chosen after three major trials at the end of March and the first two Saturdays of April. Three weeks later we flew to Amsterdam with our squad of 26 players.'

Were the victories in the pool matches as easy and convincing as the scores suggest?
'Our forwards got on top in both matches, so we had most of the possession for most of these games, and that meant both Germany and Scotland had to spend the bulk of each match defending. Although we ran up 134 points against Germany, they never gave up and kept trying to tackle us right up to the final whistle. They also managed to kick a penalty, and a couple of their players were so excited at scoring against us they ran back down the field doing rather spectacular back flips. Scotland were much more competitive, but for some inexplicable reason they made the strange decision to rest all their top players and they picked a complete reserve side against us. They made a game of it for the first half an hour, but in the end, without overstretching ourselves, we won very easily.'

How difficult were the knockout stages?
'We were surprised at how quick and skilful the Spanish were, and the difference between our teams was mainly one of physique. They were not only small in the backs but their forwards were not as big or strong or as heavy as our pack. But they made up for lack of size with a fierce determination and plenty of speed, and we were quite relieved to beat them 46-3.

'Most of the team felt the semi-final against England would be one of the hardest matches of the tournament, and it certainly looked that way when England led 6-0 midway through the first half and at half-time we only led 10-6. But our backs were too strong for them, with both Annaleah Rush and Vanessa Cootes outstanding, and we came out quite comfortable winners in the end by 44 points to 11. Our closest match was the final against America, but even though they were very competitive and well organised and really focused we were always in control and won 44-12.'

What is your favourite memory of the 1998 World Cup?
'I have all sorts of highlights from the most exciting two weeks of my rugby life, and it is hard to pick out just one. Beating the 1994 world champions, England, was a very special moment for all of our team, but that was eclipsed by actually winning the final, and I suppose the supreme moment has to be lifting the World Cup above my head. That was the crowning moment of a three-year dream. The dream had become a reality and it really sank in afterwards in the changing room. I just looked around and saw all the happy,

smiling faces of my team-mates, and I knew that was a moment we would all look back on in the years to come as something very special. Curiously enough, perhaps the most interesting statistic, which meant an enormous amount to everyone in the squad, was the news that folk back home in New Zealand were so pleased that we had reached the final that they were outraged to hear the final would not be shown live on television. It clashed exactly with the FA Cup final at Wembley between Arsenal and Newcastle United. A campaign was launched and the decision of the television company was changed. Our game was shown live, and the soccer from Wembley was shown immediately afterwards. We were delighted to learn that five times as many New Zealanders watched the Women's World Cup final as the FA Cup final.

'The impact of our triumph was such that when the plane with the team landed back in New Zealand a huge crowd had gathered at the airport. The biggest thrill of all was the fact that Jonah Lomu had travelled to the airport to greet us and offer his personal congratulations. That meant a great deal to everyone.

'The other memories the New Zealanders had were shared by all the 16 participating teams. Each had their own highlights, like Kazakhstan beating both Wales and Ireland or Spain beating Wales and France. But above all, everyone enjoyed the whole atmosphere of an unforgettable fortnight. Old friendships were renewed and new friendships were made. It was a great experience for everyone, and the only disappointment is that it will be four years before the next World Cup is scheduled.

'Such a gap is acceptable in the men's game because they have so many other international matches and tours to accommodate. But for the Kiwi ladies, all we can be sure of is playing Australia once a year. My final thought as I got on the plane back to Auckland was how nice and how appropriate it would be to have a World Cup every three years at worst or every two years at best.'

The Gal Blacks celebrate a World Cup triumph accomplished with power and skill. Can any side catch up with New Zealand before the next World Cup in four years' time?

ITALY: ready for the year 2000

BY CHRIS THAU

Former Wallaby No. 8 Julian Gardner holds the opposition at bay during Italy's victory over Scotland at the start of 1998.

After collecting the scalps of France, Ireland and Scotland and coming close to beating Wales, who narrowly escaped the fate of their Celtic cousins at Llanelli on 7 February 1998, Italy coach Georges Coste was still adamant that the 1994 thriller against Australia in Brisbane was the turning point for Italian rugby. Indeed, until July 1994, Italy beating Australia, the reigning world champions, sounded like fiction.

However, Coste' men proved Down Under not only that they are capable of competing against the best in the world but more significantly that they could play 80 minutes of sustained high-pressure rugby, something they simply could not do prior to their Australian tour. Italy restated their credentials with ferocious determination against both the Pumas and England in the RWC '95 Tournament, yet the anticlimax against Western Samoa, when they lost both shape and concentration after a promising start, underlined the fact that they had yet to exorcise some demons from their system. So are Italy ready for the Five Nations in the year 2000? The answer is yes, but…

Playing-wise, Italy vintage 2000 are comparatively superior to France in 1910, when the French joined the then Four Nations. With the exception of an accidental win over Scotland in 1911, it took France more than a decade to establish themselves. Last year, Italy beat France – admittedly still daydreaming after the Grand Slam – for the first time ever. Stirring wins over Ireland and Scotland and the scorcher against Wales at the beginning of February followed this. The catalyst that has set Italy on their way to high performance is without doubt the Rugby World Cup. While the RWC has changed the perception of rugby as a pastime, it has also provided aspiring rugby nations with a stage on which to display their prowess, and a yardstick with which to measure their progress.

RWC has helped to concentrate the minds of most rugby nations, the Italians in particular. In 1987 Italy, demolished by the rampant All Blacks in the opening game, would have reached the quarter-finals but for Gaetaniello's inexplicable knock-on in front of the Argentinian posts. They beat eventual quarter-finalists Fiji 17-15 in Dunedin, but the then coach, Marco Bollesan, would have acknowledged that his players were not really ready for the big jump. In the following tournament the Italians, coached by Frenchman Bertrand Fourcade, pushed their former tormentors New Zealand all the way, while in 1995, this time with Coste at the helm, they nailed Argentina and exposed

Wherever we play the game . . .

CLIFFORD CHANCE

200 Aldersgate Street, London EC1A 4JJ
Telephone: 0171 600 1000   Fax: 0171 600 5555
www: http://www.cliffordchance.com

...our attack is as good as our defence

At Clifford Chance, we provide a full range of legal services, from London and 23 business and commercial centres around the world.

CLIFFORD CHANCE

200 Aldersgate Street, London EC1A 4JJ
Telephone: 0171 600 1000   Fax: 0171 600 5555
www: http://www.cliffordchance.com

Georges Coste has coached Italy to some famous victories. His objective of building a strong national squad has been helped by the entry of Italian clubs into European competitions.

Massimo Cuttita (at front), in action for Harlequins last season, is one of a number of Italian internationals gaining experience with big European clubs.

England's defensive frailties, which were fully exploited by the All Blacks in the semi-finals.

During the past five seasons Coste has succeeded in developing a hard core of formidable competitors, among whom his charismatic captain, Massimo Giovanelli, has played a pivotal role. In the Frenchman's attempt to change the approach to training and the '*domani*' mentality of the Italian players, Giovanelli has been his ally and agent of influence. Giovanelli missed the 1995 RWC following a severe injury sustained in a car crash the previous year. The surgeons told him that he might never be able to walk properly again, let alone play rugby. He begged to differ, and after several months of rehabilitation, to the astonishment of his doctors and friends, he recommenced his rugby career.

Giovanelli succeeded in regaining his place in, and the captaincy of, the national team, while developing a full professional career. He and the hard-tackling centre Cristian Stoica play in Narbonne; loose-head prop Massimo Cuttitta is a London Harlequins regular, while his twin brother Marcello has again been approached by a leading English club with an offer he might be unable to refuse; the uniquely gifted fly half Diego Dominguez is orchestrating the talented back division of French club champions Stade Français; and the tough Sicilian flanker Orazio Arrancio has been playing

for Toulon. To be perfectly honest I would not be surprised if the other Italian striker Paolo Vaccari as well as the rugged former Wallaby No. 8 Julian Gardner followed their fellow professionals overseas.

The participation of Italian clubs in European club competitions has served Coste well and he has developed a second-string team ready to step into the footsteps of his regulars when the time is ripe. Some of the understudies, however, are not in the same class as their first-team colleagues and this was exposed against Croatia in the RWC qualifying rounds, when five first-team incumbents missed the match. Coste is perfectly aware of the relative strengths and weaknesses of his squad, and he has made the creation of a solid pyramid supporting the first team a priority.

In addition to talent and playing expertise, the Italians have the required infrastructure to sustain a successful Five Nations campaign. The year 2000 will add Rome to the much-sought-after rugby destinations of Paris and Dublin. The Italians have the quality stadia to host the three home matches, and the airports, hotels and restaurants to entertain tens of thousands of tourists. Television in this soccer-mad country is rugby's Achilles heel, but international success, high-profile opposition and constant exposure in the Six Nations will help FIR to project the profile of rugby throughout Italy and ultimately secure the TV support the game deserves.

Massimo Giovanelli (centre) in conversation with referee David Davies during the Italy v Scotland clash in January 1998. Seriously injured in a car accident, Giovanelli has recovered to regain the captaincy of his country.

COUNTDOWN TO 1999

BY **CHRIS THAU**

By the end of the year, more precisely 5 December 1998, 18 of the 20 Rugby World Cup (RWC) finalists will have qualified. The remaining two will be determined through a process of re-qualification, commonly known as repechage, by the end of April 1999. Of the finalists, four qualify automatically: South Africa, the holders; New Zealand, the runners-up; France, the winners of the play-off; and Wales, the hosts.

Ninety qualifying matches have been played since the RWC 1999 kicked off in the Baltic city of Riga on 28 September 1996, and a further 33 will be played in seven qualifying tournaments in Argentina, Australia, Morocco, Singapore, England, Ireland and Scotland between 15 August and 5 December. Only 25 unions from the original field of 65 have remained in contention, with a further cull due in the autumn. Fourteen teams go through to the 1999 tournament: winners Africa; winners Asia; winners, runners-up and third place Pacific; winners, runners-up and third place Americas; winners and runners-up Europe 1, 2 and 3 . However, seven of the 11 also-rans – runners-up Asia, runners-up Africa, fourth Americas, fourth Pacific, and third Europe 1, 2 and 3 – are given a second bite of the cherry at the Repechage Tournament in the spring of 1999, when the last two qualifiers will be determined.

In Europe the harsh Continental winter brought the qualifying process to a temporary halt, but after the enforced break the battle for places in the next round gathered momentum. With 33 unions involved, Europe has more teams participating than any other zone in RWC. Two Round A qualifiers, Croatia and Ukraine, found themselves playing for high stakes against leading continental powers of the likes of Italy, Romania and Russia. Croatia, having secured the services of several New Zealanders of Croatian descent, including former All Blacks Frano Botica and Matthew Cooper, gave Italy a good run for their money in their final pool match in Makarska, while Ukraine made Romania suffer in Odessa before they too succumbed.

A Croatian win over Italy would have secured the former Yugoslav republic passage into the next round at the expense of Georgia, a rugby power that has emerged from the ruins of the former Soviet empire. The Georgians, who have made considerable progress since their previous RWC outing in Sopot, Poland, in 1993, successfully challenged Russia for a place in the next round, in which they take on Romania and Ireland. All three of these East European nations – Ukraine, Georgia

Tonga's scrum half feeds during the Pacific encounter with the Cook Islands at Nuku'alofa.

Both Spain and Portugal qualified from their group. Spain (in yellow) were stronger on paper, but the Portuguese were no pushover.

and Croatia – are newly emerged on the world map and use sport in general and rugby in particular to assert their aspirations and national identity. 'For nearly a century the idea of a Ukrainian nation was anathema to the communist Soviet Union, and many people paid with their freedom, or even life, [for] any attempt to talk about a free and independent Ukraine. To play for the independent Ukraine today is a bonus, and our players are genuinely proud to represent their country. I am delighted with our performance in the last game against Romania. We showed them that we mean business and that very soon, given resources and expertise, we can be among the top continental powers,' said Viatcheslav Kalitenko, the manager of Ukraine.

The shell-shocked Russians, defeated by both Croatia and Georgia, went back to the drawing board for the second consecutive RWC. There is no doubt that Russian rugby is suffering the ill effects of the economic crisis ravaging the country, but the Russians still need to reappraise their approach to the game, both technically and tactically, in order to capitalise on their formidable athleticism. The centre of gravity of Russian rugby has moved from European Russia to Siberia, where finance and resources are available to support the game. However, the main rugby nurseries are in Russia proper, Moscow in particular, and with the loss of Ukraine and Georgia – two of the main rugby centres of the former Soviet Union – the future of the game in Russia is in jeopardy.

The Georgians have made considerable progress lately. They have improved the continuity of their game as well as their ball management and retention. Significantly their discipline – in the past their Achilles heel – has improved beyond recognition. Georgia's success at the expense of Russia has obviously added some flavour to their achievement, and the feeling in Tbilisi at the end of the qualifying match against the former imperial power was 'ecstatic' according to a local journalist.

The Georgian pool was undoubtedly the toughest in Europe, and the performance of Denmark, who nearly beat Georgia in Copenhagen, must be seen in this context. The Danes have made great progress in developing a national infrastructure, a recruitment programme and a system of elite promotion and development. According to one of their star players, the 6ft 8in giant Michael Jeppesen, who plays for Manawatu in New Zealand, they will be a power to be reckoned with in a couple of years.

The Netherlands have experienced a new lease of life under former All Black Geoff Old. The Dutch, captained by the ageless Mats Marcker, beat both Ukraine and Poland for the runners-up position in their pool and the right to play in the third European round against the likes of Italy and England. 'I guess the draw has been rather unkind to us, but the guys have to learn to play real rugby against real teams,' said coach Old after the draw. Rumour has it that the Dutch might be reinforced in the autumn by a handful of South Africans of Dutch descent, including former Sprinbgbok Adriaan Richter. 'One thing is sure – we are not going to be pushed around by the big guys,' says Old.

In the other European pool, Germany, arguably one of the most improved teams of 1997, failed in their declared attempt to reach the last nine in Europe. They lost narrowly to both Spain and Portugal, and on both occasions the dominant Germans failed to capitalise on their forward control, while giving away easy interception tries. The influence of Hans Scriba, the Natal utility back, in harnessing the talent of the German backs has been significant, but the lack of experience of the youngsters playing outside him doomed Germany's better efforts.

Spain and Portugal qualified from the pool in that order, but the Portuguese, orchestrated by their talented fly half Nuno Mourao, gave the nominally stronger Spaniards a very good run for their money. The Portuguese might relish the chance of playing Spain again in the third round, this time on neutral ground at Murrayfield.

In the Africa zone, Tunisia suffered at the hands of a rampant Zimbabwe in Bulawayo. They then beat Namibia in Tunis, only to miss the boat as Namibia scored an injury-time try to beat Zimbabwe in Windhoek. The three teams finished equal on points, but with more tries scored, Zimbabwe and Namibia went through to round four.

The first of this year's qualifying tournaments kicks off in Argentina in August. It involves the hosts, the United States, Canada and the winners of Round B, Uruguay. Uruguay, say eye-witnesses, were lucky to go through at the expense of a brave and inventive Chile, and it will be interesting to see if skipper Diego Ormaechea – at the end of his career – will be able to skipper 'Los Terros' to a place among the top three.

Papenfus brings the ball away for Zimbabwe during their victory over Tunisia at Bulawayo.

performance

from

N E X T

PERSONAL REFLECTIONS

MICHAEL LYNAGH TALKS TO NIGEL STARMER-SMITH

*O*f all the players who have been recruited to the colours of an English club in the professional era, none has been more successful and none more popular than Australian fly half Michael Lynagh. He joined Saracens in the summer of 1996, together with Philippe Sella, as the first element of the club's determination to project itself from homely, if unfashionable, family unit in North London to major player on the national stage, following Nigel Wray's £2 million investment.

Lynagh arrived after a career that encompassed 72 caps for Australia between 1984 and 1995; the captaincy of his country; a world record 911 points in international rugby; more than 100 appearances for Queensland; Queensland Club Premiership titles with his university; successive Italian Club Championship titles with Treviso; and appearances in every game bar one (v Romania in 1995) for Australia in all three World Cups. His first competitive outing for the 'Men in Black' came in the humble surroundings of Enfield Football Club on 31 August 1996 and proved to be an auspicious beginning. Lynagh kicked five penalty goals and a conversion in the club's first-ever league victory over Leicester.

Saracens finished sixth in the league that season, but Lynagh's appearances were disrupted by injury. Last season, and with the club now ground-sharing with Watford FC, he played a crucial role in sustaining Saracens' challenge for the Allied Dunbar Premiership title through to the final day of the championship, the club finishing in second place, just one point behind Newcastle. However, there was confirmation of Saracens' new-found status as one of the top two English clubs when they won the knockout competition, the Tetley's Bitter Cup, for the very first time.

To me, since I first saw him play in the colours of the all-conquering Australian Schoolboys side of 1981-82 (as a centre, alongside Papworth, Burke and Knox, with Tuynman as captain) he has been the model player as amateur and professional – not just because of his outstanding talent at club and international level but because he also happens to be the most modest, charming and likeable person to have graced the rugby stage.

Michael Lynagh hung up his boots in May this year, after 16 years of senior rugby.

Michael Lynagh kicks for goal during the 1991 World Cup final against England, won by Australia by 12 points to 6.

Man of the Match Lynagh celebrates after Saracens' 48-18 victory over Wasps to win the Tetley's Bitter Cup. With him are try scorer and fellow Australian Ryan Constable and, holding the cup, François Pienaar.

When I arrived at Southgate, my ambitions were uncomplicated: from a rugby point of view, to play well and to help put Saracens on the map. So I guess that in winning the Tetley's Bitter Cup and coming second in the league championship we really achieved that. But it's not the end of the road, more the start for the club. It is very satisfying to sit back and say I was part of it all.

When I first arrived at Saracens, I saw it as very much like one of our Australian clubs – a small suburban ground, a lot of players moving on to more fashionable, and successful, clubs, but now I look back and reflect that we are one of the few clubs who seem to have got it right. We have excellent facilities at Watford. Spectators enjoy the stadium and are well looked after, helping to make what was comparatively a rugby desert into something of a hotbed of the game. And for the most part our playing style has been very attractive to watch.

Popularising the game in Watford has not come about by chance or just good luck. We have worked hard. Every week, for instance, we have a roster requiring players to go out into the community – whether hospitals or schools, opening new business premises and so on, really integrating ourselves into the local scene. When a sporting team arrives in a new environment, invariably they ask local people to come and watch, but very rarely do the team or club put something back into the community. We see it as a two-way street, and I believe that has been an important element in our success. The arrival of Peter Deakin as Marketing Director was a key factor, with his experience in the league game, and as players we recognise our responsibilities and have come to enjoy developing relationships with people in the town of Watford. Now that we have established that rapport in the immediate vicinity we are hoping to branch out further into pockets around North London – Enfield, Southgate (where we still train), Barnet and so on. It is important that we give something back.

On the field there were many elements to our playing success. The club recruited well and acquired not only players of outstanding talent but individuals who would integrate well and develop a team spirit: players like Philippe [Sella], the Wallaces, Ryan Constable, Paddy Johns and, of course, François Pienaar. It can't have been that easy for François, probably the second most famous and revered South African after Nelson Mandela, to arrive in Southgate and to settle and then contribute to the club as much as he has. They all blended well to a squad which could also boast the home-grown talent of such as Tony Diprose, Richard Hill, Kyran Bracken, Ben Sturnham and Danny Grewcock. We got decision makers in key positions – half back [scrum half], No. 8 and fly half. That was important. And we enjoyed good all round talent in the playing squad, with quality cover in depth. We were lucky this past season in not sustaining too many injuries to key players and we had a good squad system, introduced by François, which prevented overplaying particular individuals by ringing the changes and making use of the replacement system, and that worked well for us.

The club's long-standing reputation for producing back-row forwards has been maintained, and it was rewarding this season to see the development of Ben Sturnham, taking over from Richard Hill who suffered severely from back injury problems. Ben's a player for the future – alas no longer with Saracens – but he's still got a long way to go and some learning to do. He's a very imposing figure, very quick, but needs to improve his distribution of the ball after he has made breaks, whilst in defence he needs to make more of an impact. Now he's going to Bath, and I just hope that his development can continue, because he learned a lot under François, who really set him on his way. Tony Diprose enjoyed a really good year, and I was glad to see him back in the England Test team. He is a very talented player. People talk about his ball skills, but importantly he's also quite a competitive person and pretty physical – and of course he's a Saracen through and through.

I started contemplating my rugby future – or lack of it! – last November during the season and spoke about it with my family. To be honest, I think my wife Isabella would have been perfectly happy – perhaps happier – for me to have carried on playing. But I've had enough and I want to go on and do some other things. I had the option to play on with Saracens, but they were very supportive of my decision. I'm happy that I've finished now. Physically the game was beginning to take its toll – pre-

Michael Lynagh announces his retirement. 'I think my wife Isabella would have been perfectly happy – perhaps happier – for me to have carried on playing. But I've had enough,' says Lynagh.

Lynagh ships the ball on as Gary Rees prepares to pounce during the England v Australia international of the Wallabies 1984 Grand Slam tour.

season preparation, which had never been a problem for me, actually was quite a tough ordeal. The thought of going through that again did not appeal. The most difficult thing of all for me was the tension and the nervous energy before each game. People may be surprised I say that, but it is very relevant with goal-kicking a major responsibility to carry. After 16 years of top-level rugby, that was beginning to wear a bit thin, too.

My original plans were based on the fact that I would come to play in England for between three and five years – though I said to Nigel Wray at the outset that five years might be a bit long, so the arrangement was always flexible. We shall stay in London. We like living here, and the work opportunities in my field of real estate are enormous. I've been at work for one week as I speak, and so far, so good. Add to that the opportunity to visit Wimbledon or attend a Lord's Test match, and the attraction of London is so obvious to someone who as a kid in Australia could only dream of such things. And for Isabella, we're not far from her family home in Italy (less close to my Australian roots, of course!). I'm quite happy here. We'll see what happens.

I am often asked if I am glad to have played most of my rugby in the amateur era. To a certain extent, yes. I consider myself very fortunate to have enjoyed rugby in the 1980s. Perhaps that was the best time of all, when tours were two and half months long, and I was a student able to travel the world with 30 of your friends in tow, playing international rugby. Not a bad scene! Now with the professional era, I've benfited from that too. I have to question, though, whether I would have been keen to join the professional game had I been starting out now. I'm glad to have been to university and to have already worked within a career in real estate which I can now return to. It's a major problem now for professional rugby that youngsters are leaving school, being contracted to a club over here or to a province in the southern hemisphere, never having entered tertiary education and never having worked, and facing the prospect of a limited span of time as a player. The life span of a top rugby player is short, and becoming increasingly shorter, because of the number of games played and their intensity.

So at the age of 28 or 29, the reality for many will be the end of a playing career and no obvious working-career openings ahead. The pay does not equate to that of top soccer professionals, where players may be in a position to retire if they have invested wisely. So what do the ex-rugby players do? It is a real concern. I know that at Saracens, where we bring in youngsters on contracts, we do our best to ensure that they do some study and career training as well. You cannot practise rugby all day and every day, and you must do something other than squander your time playing video games.

I have also been asked many a time about the present state of English rugby and its administrative problems. The essential difference, when you compare England with the southern hemisphere, is the ownership of the players. In Australia, New Zealand and South Africa, it is with the union – the Australian RFU, then Queensland or New South Wales and so on, from the top down. Over here, it seems the RFU missed the boat by allowing the clubs to contract the players first. Hence the cause of the enormous problem between club and country. I can only hope international rugby is able to continue, and continues to thrive here in England.

Having got Australia through to the semi-finals with his score against Ireland, Lynagh helped his country go all the way to victory in the 1991 World Cup. Here he shares a moment of glory with Simon Poidevin.

I believe club rugby can continue to progress. The number of spectators is certainly increasing, so the clubs must be doing something right. What we have to ensure is that the clubs prosper while England, Ireland, Scotland and Wales do not diminish in status or importance at international level. There are solutions, but tough decisions are required. Club rugby must be played on a regular weekly basis, and if England play on Saturday, then the club games should be on the Sunday. This would mean that given the obvious priority of the national side the availability to Saracens of someone like Tony Diprose would be reduced by eight or nine weekends a season. Saracens would therefore reduce his salary accordingly, but Tony would not lose out as England would make up the difference. Thus the club's financial responsibilities are lessened and the money 'saved' by the club can be invested in an understudy who covers for Tony. This would achieve several objectives: the availability of the best players for England, the continuity of the club's league programme and a reduction in the club's financial liabilities to its leading players.

I also believe that there are too many competitions. We have the European Cup, the Tetley's Bitter Cup, the Allied Dunbar league, the Five Nations tournament and the recently added Cook Cup [England v Australia, home and away]. I would be tempted to combine the knockout cup and the league and do as happens in the Sydney Rugby League competition, where the top clubs at the end of the league season play off, on a knockout basis, for the cup – with the final at Twickenham. I am aware that this eliminates the possibility of any giant-killing acts by junior clubs, but so be it. As I said, there are tough decisions to be made for the future wellbeing of the game, and that is top priority. I want England and English club rugby to enjoy their day in the sun – well, there were a few days like that this season!

A remarkable career draws to a close. World record international points scorer and master fly half Michael Lynagh pictured in his last match for Saracens, against Northampton on 14 May 1998.

As for my own favourite 'day in the sun', from all those games on so many different rugby grounds around the world, my most cherished moment would have to be the World Cup quarter-final against Ireland in Dublin in 1991. I was acting captain that day. We went behind when Gordon Hamilton scored a remarkable Irish try, and I managed to engineer and score the decisive score in the final seconds of the match. As a particular moment, when it really counted, that one is unsurpassed for me. We met New Zealand in the semi-finals a week later, and the Wallabies' first-half display was probably the best that I have ever been involved in. In the second half, our defence was outstanding and I guess that was when we really began to believe that this would be our World Cup. Defence was the key to winning the final at Twickenham. We had about 40 per cent of the ball, England had the rest and we had to stand there and tackle to win.

I've had many wonderful days and victories with Australia, Queensland and Saracens – not forgetting Treviso. In fact winning the Italian Club Championship with them in my first year will stand as one of my treasured memories, mainly because of the cultural differences I had to adjust to, a new language and a different style of rugby all combining to make the experience very special.

I have no complaint. It's been so much fun.'

THE WORLD'S GREATEST RUGBY SHOW

BY **CHRIS THAU**

An inspired French scribe has put it in a nutshell: 'Amazingly Irish – the salt and pepper of rugby.' Indeed, by winning the 30th World Junior Championship, the Irish added spice to a competition dulled by a combination of French and Argentinian supremacy. The fact that on their way to the top they knocked out both reigning champions Argentina and hosts France gave their success additional flavour. Ireland, on their second appearance in the tournament, become the sixth nation after France, Argentina, Romania, Italy and South Africa to have their name engraved on the wooden *Bouclier* in the 30-year history of this annual event. The Irish success was not an accident. It was a clear statement of talent, vitality and expertise, seasoned with traditional Irish ingredients – fire and brimstone.

Ireland's Shane Moore receives the Junior World Championship trophy from FIRA President Jean-Claude Baqué.

The Irish started the campaign against the US Eagles Juniors, who were making their debut in the tournament, and found themselves trailing 0-7 after some five minutes in Lombez. The lively Americans tackled and ran hard and put the Irish under pressure at the outset, but once Ireland took control of the line out through their outstanding duo Donnacha O'Callaghan and Damien Broughall – a pairing regarded by the pundits as one of Ireland's trump cards in the tournament – and sorted out their early midfield blues, there was very little the gallant Americans could do to stem the Irish tide.

The crunch for the Irish came against a talented and fired-up baby Springboks side who by half-time seemed set to run away with the match. Trailing by 17-0 at the break, the Irish seemed unable to match South Africa's pounds, inches or speed of thought and limb. Whatever coaches Declan Kidney and Bart Fannin told the youngsters at half-time is immaterial. Suffice it to say that in the second half the Irish subjected their South African tormentors to the same treatment they had to put up with during the first 35 minutes.

The match ended 17-17, with Ireland losing the ensuing penalty shoot-out 4-3. However, the South Africans paid dearly for using one of their reserve players – who was on the bench at the end of the match – for the penalty shoot-out. The Irish lodged a complaint, and the organisers promptly demoted South Africa, giving the match to Ireland.

Midland Bank is pleased to be associated with Wooden Spoon Society Rugby World '99.

Midland Bank
Member HSBC *Group*

The rest is history, with the Irish improving both in quality and confidence as the tournament wore on. It is difficult to single out any particular player in what, by and large, was a superb team effort, but the dispatches after the hard-fought semi-final win over Argentina and the sizzling final against France mentioned hooker Aidan Kearney, captain courageous Shane Moore and his centre partner Brian O'Driscoll, as well as the half-back partnership of Ciaran Campbell and Paddy Wallace, who between them controlled the games with growing authority. The generous French public gave the Irish youngsters a standing ovation at the end of an historic encounter at the Sept Deniers Stadium in Toulouse.

As the Irish and the South Africans respectively put the United States and Poland to sword in the first round, elsewhere the tournament kicked off with three upsets, with Wales, Scotland and Romania – all three legitimate contenders to places in the last four – losing their opening matches. For Wales, hosts for the 31st tournament in 1999, winning their second match, after the 23-19 shock defeat by Canada, became a matter of survival. Another defeat, at the hands of the Scots, who were also battling to avoid relegation after their surprise defeat by Chile, would have sentenced them to the ignominy of having to play in the second division in front of their own public in 1999. In the magnificent Rodez Stadium in front of nearly 10,000 knowledgeable spectators, the Welsh youngsters, inspired by captain Gareth Bowen, raised themselves to the occasion and managed to overcome a strong and committed Scotland 20-7 after a hard and uncompromising battle.

Japan (in hoops) surprised Spain with both their organisation and skill.

In the first round Chile, who were promoted from the second division this year, surprisingly beat Scotland, who were reportedly unprepared for the South Americans' firebrand 15-man rugby. Chile then naively lost in the second round to an athletic but limited Canadian team in the dying seconds of a fast and entertaining game. If their discipline would match their ball skills and natural affinity for the game, the Chileans could become a force to be reckoned with. They finished seventh – their highest position in the tournament so far – and had the satisfaction of beating arch rivals Uruguay 14-13 in the play-off for seventh place, the first time ever that Chile had beaten their neighbours.

The format of the tournament is designed to allow the maximum number of teams (34 this year) to compete in a short space of time (one week). The teams are divided into divisions and play knockout matches in these divisions from round one. The first-round winners go on playing against each other in the top half of the table, while the losers also carry on playing among themselves in the bottom half. This format places great emphasis on winning the first match, which explains how Uruguay, who beat Romania on day one but lost all three matches afterwards, finished eighth, ahead of Wales (ninth), who lost their first match but won all their three subsequent encounters.

Japan, who lost their opening match against France, showed glimpses of their tremendous potential in their second-round win over Spain, while Romania, traditionally very strong in this age group, avenged their unexpected first-round defeat by Uruguay with a thorough demolition of Russia in round two. Poland recovered from their 93-3 annihilation at the hands of South Africa – the highest score of the competition – to beat the United States and secure their survival in the first division for 1999. Italy, who beat Spain 20-10 in their opening match, then lost 8-37 to France in the second round. However, the young Italians gave France a far tougher game than the score suggests.

Rumour among senior IRB and FIRA officials has it that next year in Wales the three missing forces of international junior rugby – New Zealand, England and Australia – are likely to join the competition, along with a host of other nations keen to get exposure for their younger generation at this level. Based on this year's precedent of Japan, Canada and the United States being placed directly in division one, if the three do apply to join the tournament, they will most likely also gain direct entry to the first division. That means that the bottom four teams from this year – the United States, Spain, Russia and Scotland – will be relegated to division two to accommodate the three newcomers. This will force a purge of similar magnitude at the bottom of division two, unless the organisers decide to enlarge it from eight to 16 nations to take into account the four relegated sides and other new unions keen to enter the tournament. Until this year the tournament had been of a manageable size, but its success, based in part on the IRB decision to part-fund travel and accommodation costs, has brought into the picture many unions that were previously unaware of its existence or unable to raise the necessary finance to send a side.

IRB chairman Vernon Pugh QC had the following to say on the subject: 'The IRB/FIRA Rugby Junior World Championship is a great event and the IRB support has helped some of the Unions, previously unable to attend, to raise a team to participate. We hope that in 1999 in Wales all leading playing nations will have entered a team. But the success of the Tournament has brought with it certain problems, most of them of logistic in nature. It has been said that the optimal structure of the Tournament is based on a three-division, 32-nations format, largely similar to the event in France this year. As I understand, the

The Argentinian scrum half gets the ball away during the third-place play-off match against Canada.

number of applicants for 1999 has already gone from 34 to over 40. It is essential that we find a balance between the development requirements of the IRB members and the need to protect and nurture the Tournament to its optimal format.'

Given the large gap in standards, ability and development between the participating unions, the divisional structure of the Junior World Championship is a great advantage. The teams are split into three divisions – in fact this year there was a fourth, comprising just Switzerland and Luxembourg – which operate on a promotion-relegation basis. This system enables the aspiring unions to build up their strength in depth gradually and move up the ladder once they are ready to confront the stronger teams. The case of Chile is a good example. Having won the second division last year, they finished in the top eight in 1998.

Ukraine winning the aerial battle against Chinese Taipei in the third division final.

In the final of the second division, Georgia beat Portugal 25-7. The Georgians were coached by one of the legendary figures of Georgian rugby, David Kilasonia, helped this year by New Zealand expert Brad Meurat, who was flown over to Tbilisi by one of the multinationals building the TransCaucasian oil pipeline. Meanwhile, Ukraine – coached by an enduring hero of Ukrainian rugby, Igor Bobkov, won the third division against a resourceful and inventive Chinese Taipei team. Obviously the standards vary greatly between the lower divisions and the top eight in the first division. However, the divisional format ensures balanced matches at all levels, despite the technical shortcomings of the participants.

This is why the Georgians' clash with Germany in round one of the second division was an attractive and well-balanced encounter, while the Belgian win over a resourceful Morocco was warmly applauded by the appreciative crowd. The same comments were valid for division three, where the participants, Cote d'Ivoire, Brazil, Croatia, Andorra, Bulgaria, Chinese Taipei, Sweden and Ukraine, gave a good account of themselves.

The tournament was superbly organised by FIRA and the Midi-Pyrenees Committee of the French Federation. The organising team led by FIRA President Jean-Claude Baqué left no stone unturned in their attempt to help the 34 delegations sample traditional French hospitality and enjoy the tournament, the biggest and best-run in the event's 30-year history. The Welsh Rugby Union, the organisers of the 31st championship during the 1999 Easter break, are faced with a huge challenge as they prepare to host the 1999 senior RWC in the autumn.

HEINZ

MEANZ

TRIEZ

A GREAT SUPPORTER OF WORLD RUGBY

CLUBS AND CUPS

FALCONS FLYING HIGH

ROB ANDREW TALKS TO NIGEL STARMER-SMITH

Newcastle Director of Rugby and fly half Rob Andrew in action against Richmond in the Falcons title-winning 1997-98 season.

Rob Andrew, Director of Rugby of Allied Dunbar Premiership Champions Newcastle, talks to Nigel Starmer-Smith about the club's recipe for success and where they go from here.

What have been the key ingredients of Newcastle's success?
'I would point to two things. First, as a team we have done the basics very well. It starts up front, and effectively the forwards won us the championship. Our line-out play was good, our ball retention very good and we defended really well. Secondly, our success owes much to our desire to win, and that was epitomised in tight matches when we worked hard to hold on to narrow leads and so win critical games. When you think back to those league wins which were by a margin of ten points or less – against Richmond, Leicester, Gloucester, Northampton (twice), Saracens and Bath – and the fact that we won the title by being just one point ahead of Saracens, you realise just how significant each of those results proved to be.'

Newcastle seemed to have developed more rapidly than most clubs an efficient 'behind-the-scenes' structure.
'We've come a long way in less than three years and we're still working on it. The first season was spent 'bedding-in' with what we had. That was sufficient to gain us the necessary promotion to Division 1. As a result we now have a good first-choice side, but, as this close season has shown, nothing stands still, and I'm sure the arrival of Marius Hurter, the Springbok prop, and young additions from the North of England with England Under 21 experience Peter Massy, Michael Wood and Ian Peel will be helpful. Of course we recognise the contributions to our success that Pat Lam and Alan Tait have made – players of that calibre are not readily replaced, but change is a natural part of the professional game.

'It is, however, important to recognise the need to develop young players alongside the experienced and established stars that we have like Ryan, Weir, Popplewell, Armstrong, Nesdale, Tuigamala, Graham and Underwood. The new youngsters for this season are very exciting players who are joining the Premiership champions to further their careers. As part of this focus on developing new talent we also have in place good connections with the local universities, Newcastle University, Durham and Northumbria – three excellent places of learning that attract a lot of promising rugby players, and this has been of great benefit to Jonny Wilkinson, Martin Shaw and Stuart Legg. We're trying to keep the momentum going.

'Our coaching structure has been effective. You cannot run a first–class rugby team with one person. As well as being a player, I fulfil the role of team manager whilst Dean Ryan and Steve Bates take the principal credit for coaching the side, with a team selection that is appropriate to meet whoever it is that we are playing against. Dean is effectively the forwards coach, as well as being a playing member of the squad, whilst Steve is in charge of the backs and oversees the whole thing. So it is a three-man team, with the important backup of Martin Brewer as physiotherapist.

'It is vital, too, to have a well-defined management structure in place, and under the club's overall chairmanship of Sir John Hall, the Executive Director David Campbell has introduced a new setup for this coming season, with John Oates assisted by Alex Jackson, who undertake responsibility for media liaison. Paul Mackinnon is Rugby Development Manager.'

You were, as a club, first off the blocks, so to speak, in terms of recruitment, following your appointment as Director of Rugby in 1995. What are your principle criteria in recruiting?

'Apart from the obvious factors – ability to perform to a sufficient standard, the ability of the individual to blend with the whole squad, and the need to bolster team strength in certain areas – for me there is one other particular area of concern, and that is team development: looking ahead. To me the art of management is about getting the right mix between senior experienced professionals and younger developing talent. It is no good having an imbalance with too many older players whose careers are coming to an end nor attempting, or expecting, to be successful with a team full of kids. It's the following season you have to look towards.'

Having achieved your initial targets so quickly, will it be difficult to maintain the momentum?

'I don't think so. We have worked hard and earned our success, first promotion, then the Premiership title, and we feel proud of what we have achieved. But in a sense, that is only the start. We need to establish Newcastle as part of the rugby landscape of our region and the country. There is no point in being up on a pedestal for a season or two; to flourish and then disappear. We want to be the Bath or Leicester of the future. Nor is it down to money. It does not matter how much you pay players, you will not achieve and maintain success unless

Newcastle's Player of the Season, Western Samoan flanker Pat Lam, on the charge against Gloucester.

there is a hunger for winning for the sake of winning. We have a team of winners, prepared to perform to their best on the field of play. There will be a few changes along the way, but we shall continue to roll the team forward and strive to be the best in the land.'

Can you see Newcastle rugby ever becoming as important to Tyneside as Newcastle soccer?
'I believe it can be, in a slightly different way. I see Newcastle RFC as a regional side, for the North of England really, not just Newcastle, extending even to Cumbria and the South of Scotland. We will be different from most. Soccer, however strong, is very localised. Sunderland and Middlesborough are nearby rivals restricting Newcastle's sphere of influence. I was watching Sunderland in their play-off with Sheffield United and was gratified and encouraged by the level of support for the Falcons that was expressed to me on that occasion, and equally in Middlesborough where I used to play. I seriously believe that there is a huge growth potential in rugby and have said many times that club rugby is sitting on a time bomb which is set to explode around us. There have been signs this season – record crowds everywhere and the Saracens experience. An interesting yardstick will be whether Richmond make a success of their move to Reading. I think there are positive indications that we can create a rugby club infrastructure which is as passionate and almost as cultlike as soccer is in this country. I think there are clear signs that it is there to be grasped.'

Captain for the day Alan Tait (far right) helps show off the Sanyo Cup after Newcastle had beaten the World XV at Twickenham. The showpiece season-closer was British Lion Tait's farewell appearance for the Falcons.

A proud Sir John Hall displays the Allied Dunbar Premiership trophy to Newcastle followers, aided by Falcons and England No. 8 Dean Ryan.

ONE NAME ALWAYS LIVES UP TO THE CHALLENGE.

What more could you ask of a major player than endurance, consistency and a world-wide reputation?

Land Rover can offer you all this and more, with Defender giving you a combination of raw strength and practicality which make it the toughest 4x4 around.

If it's all-round performance you're looking for then the Discovery can satisfy all your needs. With the choice of engines and up to seven seats, there's no better vehicle for offering complete versatility.

And nothing has earned itself a reputation as a serious 4x4 player faster than the impressive new Freelander.

To complete this winning team comes the leader of the pack, Range Rover.

And with the added advantages of Freedom Finance and, where status permits, Diplomatic concessions, we can provide the package that takes performance to new heights.

For more information call one of the numbers below.

THE BEST 4x4xFAR

BRISTOL: on the edge of extinction?

BY **ALASTAIR HIGNELL**

Bristol rugby fans are still in shock. At the start of last season, they had a first division team to support. Their club, though in debt, still owned its own ground, training pitch and car park, as well as 25 acres of land at nearby Filton. At the start of this season, relegation to the second division was the least of the fans' concerns. In the space of one horror-filled week in July, the club had first of all demanded the players take a drastic pay cut, then, before they could respond, called in the Official Receiver. A day later the club signed over its rights to the Memorial Ground. Bristol was not only bust, but down from the first division and out of what had been home for the past 77 years.

Bristol didn't even deserve the lifeline offered by the expansion of the first division for this season. Beaten 20 times in their 22 league matches, they were bundled out of the cup by a third division side, Worcester; they sacked their coach, Alan Davies; and they sold their ground to pay off their debts. It was hard to imagine a way in which matters could get worse, but it should have come as no surprise to those who knew the Memorial Ground well that Bristol should manage to find one.

It's easy for outsiders to forget the statistics that have kept Bristolians warm in the recent dark days: that just under a quarter of a century ago, Bristol won the precursor to the league championship, the Sunday Telegraph Pennant; that 15 years ago, when they beat Leicester in a thrilling cup final at Twickenham, they could justifiably claim to be the best team in England; or that 10 years ago the cup final defeat by Harlequins was their only loss in months.

By then, though, the rot had well and truly set in. The building of the Centenary Stand in that year, 1988, perfectly encapsulated the prevailing attitude at the club. Just as they had been caught unawares by the rise of Bath during the previous decade, now they were

Happier days at Bristol as skipper Mike Rafter hoists the John Player Cup in 1983.

One of too many that got away. Stuart Barnes clears for Bristol against, ironically, Bath in 1984. Barnes later joined Bristol's West Country rivals and was instrumental in their great success in the late 1980s and early 1990s.

caught unawares by the recession. Just as they had assumed that the former was a passing phase, now they assumed the latter didn't apply to them. Just as they had presumed that someone would come up with the money to pay for the stand, so they presumed that the architect knew what he was doing. What they got was a crippling debt and an ugly edifice that signally failed to fulfil its two most basic functions. Before some fairly drastic alterations were made, several rows at the front of the stand had neither the protection of the roof, nor a view of the whole pitch!

The players had already begun to vote with their feet. Bristol had once been the only serious option for ambitious rugby players arriving to work in the West Country. Gloucester were too parochial; Bath were only just better than Clifton. However, the advances at the Recreation Ground – symbolically Bath's first real tangible success was their defeat of Bristol in the 1984 cup final – left Bristol competing for players, an activity they felt they were above. So Stuart Barnes and later Jonathan Webb were allowed to head off down the A4 with little thought given to the reasons for their departures. So players like Phil de Glanville and Dave Egerton were allowed to slip through the Memorial Ground net, approached by Bristol and then ignored. So in recent years have nearly all of Bristol's successful signings been driven away. England tourist Josh Lewsey is only the latest in a long line that includes Garath Archer, Kyran Bracken, Simon Shaw and Martin Corry. But what really should have set the alarm bells ringing was the way the club managed to alienate even its favourite sons. Derek Eves and Andy Blackmore – Bristolians both, who had worked wonders in Bristol's service – took off to Coventry and took even more players with them.

Eves was one of a host of former players who watched in sadness as London Scottish finally kicked Bristol off the first division precipice in May. They saw a side still packed full of talent. Wales' most-capped scrum half Robert Jones as captain, Canadian World Cup star Al Charron and Irish flanker David Corkery in the pack, current Ireland centre Kevin Maggs operating in a back line that included former Ireland player Paul Burke and former England full back Paul Hull. Bristol needed to beat the Exiles by four points to stay in the top flight, but though several individuals played well, and though the Memorial Ground faithful did their best to impersonate a hostile crowd, the passion that had characterised Bristol's previous fights against relegation was missing. When, with Bristol leading 12-11, Burke failed to ground the ball near the Scottish posts, all the stuffing was knocked out of Bristol. They knew they had lost the battle to stay in the top flight. They knew they faced an uncertain future. They didn't know then that they'd be out of a job before they next had the chance to kick a ball in anger.

The great fear is that, even if they can survive as a club, Bristol will now go into free fall, much as Coventry and London Welsh, two other great clubs of the 1970s, did. The great hope is that a Nigel Wray or a Sir John Hall can be found; someone who with one flash of his chequebook can make all of Bristol's financial problems go away and at the same time allow Bristolians to create the modern, prosperous pro-active rugby club that the city deserves. That scenario, though, looks more and more like wishful thinking. The club spent the whole of last season promising that just such an investor was about to deliver. More than one sugar daddy, however, was put off by the size of the debt he would have to pay off before doing something positive with his millions. Another potential saviour, Amtrak Pensions, pulled out of a deal to buy the ground at the last minute when it discovered that rights to develop the training annexe had already been promised away. The deal that eventually sold the ground to tenants Bristol Rovers paid off some of a debt reckoned to be in excess of £2 million, but not all of it. Although Bristol were apparently in sounder financial shape than they had been a couple of years before, the projections for this season were still for losses of £50-60,000 per month. Those figures persuaded the club's chairman and chief creditor Arthur Holmes, who had in the past paid the players' wages out of his own pocket, to pull the plug. So Bristol, now without that crippling burden of debt, but also without very much in the way of assets except the players, drop down into the second division, while big-spenders Worcester and Leeds come up into it. With only one side guaranteed automatic promotion next year – and none the following, World Cup year – Bristol face a huge battle just to stay alive.

Former Wales scrum half Robert Jones was just one illustrious member of Bristol's highly talented back division last season.

PERFECT CURTAIN CALL:
the Tetley's Bitter final

BY **NIGEL STARMER-SMITH**

Saracens' England scrum half Kyran Bracken rifles the ball upfield. Wasps could make little impression against the array of stars, English and otherwise, fielded by the 'Men in Black'.

You could guarantee one thing concerning the 1998 Tetley's Bitter Cup final: there would be a first-time cup winner in either Saracens or Wasps. And you could just about guarantee two other things: that the game would be better to watch than the last year's dreary Twickenham encounter between Leicester and Sale, and that Lynagh and Sella were destined to depart the rugby scene in glory.

It was probably the hottest day of 1998 as rival captains Dallaglio and Diprose led their respective teams out to do battle. As one looked down upon the two teams assembled in line abreast before kick-off, and upon a 60,000 crowd, it was there for all to see in this first all-London affair: a brave England contingent (New Zealand newcomer Mark Weedon apart) decked out in the colours of Wasps against a congregation of world stars – from South Africa, New Zealand, Australia, France, Argentina and Ireland; ten players all born outside the UK – in the colours of the 'Men in Black', Saracens. For those sticklers for accuracy who may be tempted to question the veracity of this assessment, please note that Canadian international Gareth Rees (though born in Duncan, British Columbia) has Welsh parents and has been part of the English rugby scene for so long, since Harrow schooldays, that he counts as one of us; that Irish cap Rob Henderson, also of Wasps, was born in New Malden and educated in England; and that Kyran Bracken of Saracens was born in Dublin! Suffice it to say it was never going to be an even contest.

Of course, not. Nor was there any doubt who was going to run the show. Enter on to the Twickenham stage, for the last time in full-blown competition, a brace of players with the combined age of 70 – Michael Lynagh, at 34 as masterful in the arts of fly-half play as ever, the epitome of the intelligent rugby player, alongside the rugged talents of the best defensive centre of the last 16 years, still sharp, though now 36 and shorn of hair, Philippe Sella. It didn't take them very long to lay down the law that tells you that class counts, for within 13 minutes of the kick-off, Saracens were 15 points ahead. A demonstration of power and swerve, reminiscent of his heyday with France, saw Sella score the opening try – for Lynagh to convert, of course.

Moments later, a 33-yard Lynagh dropped goal soared home, before Lynagh's fellow Australian Ryan Constable put Saracens in the clear with another try. Of course, none of this could have happened so readily had not the 'Black Pack' held sway – Paul Wallace (what an influence he has been), François Pienaar (player-coach, and even more influence to boot), Danny Grewcock (ex-Coventry) and the emergent Ben Sturnham, not forgetting the presence of Tony Diprose, a soft-spoken captain whose tones belie a firm resolve. Thirteen minutes into the match, and to all intents and purposes the contest was over.

Thereafter, Wasps, as Lawrence Dallaglio admitted, could only attempt to play 'catch-up' rugby, but the players most competent at that were on the other side. Five more tries were to follow – 18-34 was the closest Wasps came to parity – and appropriately the last moment of scoring action came from Lynagh with his conversion of the final try. His calm display of skill and efficiency brought him, quite rightly, the Man of the Match award.

In defeat, there was no disgrace for Wasps, whose resilience was rewarded by tries from the dashing Roiser and the effervescent Volley, while in addition to his typically stately elegance as a performer, Gareth Rees (who had appeared in the 1986 cup final while still at Harrow School) added two penalty goals and a conversion.

The final scoreline of 48-18 created a new record aggregate score of 66 points, of which, significantly I feel, 41 points were scored by non-Englishmen. Forty-eight points by Saracens equalled Bath's record tally against Gloucester in 1990. While Wasps had three times been cup runners-up (in 1986, 1987 and 1995), Saracens had never before survived the semi-finals.

Perhaps, in retrospect, the outcome can be seen to have been preordained. It was the most fitting farewell for the retiring duo – Lynagh and Sella. In a match report, one Sunday quality newspaper rugby correspondent remarked in his opening salvo, 'Saracens made a massive statement for the health and vibrancy of English rugby.' I seldom take issue with my media colleagues. On this occasion, however, I feel bound to say, 'How wrong can you be?'

Now just remind me, who was it who scored the first 22 points for Saracens? Oh yes, a Frenchman, a South African and two Australians!

Saracens' soft-spoken but resolute skipper Tony Diprose raises aloft the Tetley's Bitter Cup, capped by the inevitable fez.

Saracens celebrate their arrival in rugby's big time with their victory in the Tetley's Bitter Cup final.

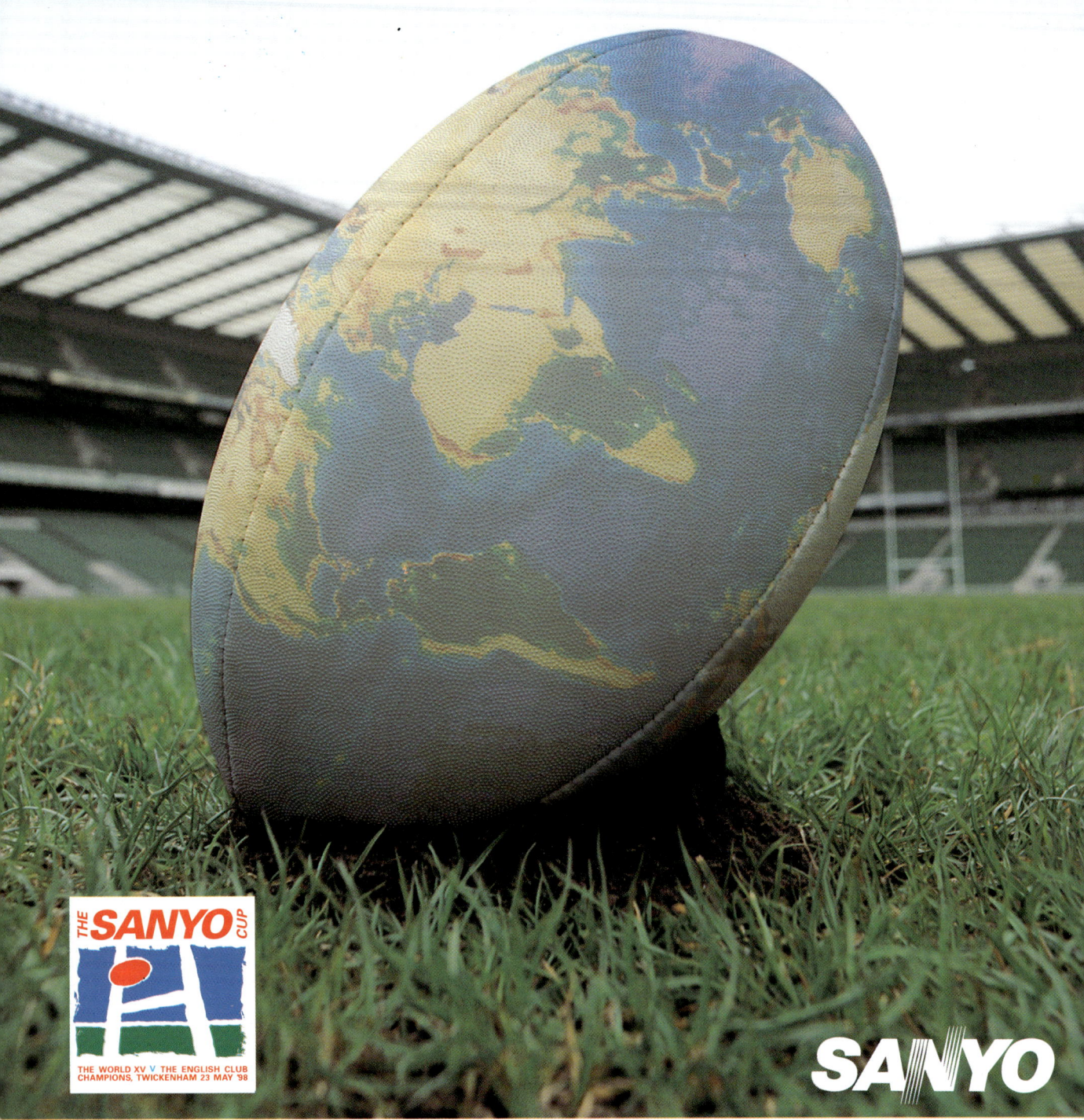

Always ahead of the pack...

THE **SANYO** CUP

THE WORLD XV V THE ENGLISH CLUB
CHAMPIONS, TWICKENHAM 23 MAY '98

SANYO

TV & Video • Digital Cameras • Camcorders • Hi-Fi • CD Portables
Microwave Ovens • Vacuum Cleaners • Commercial Products

LIGHT IN THE DARKNESS: the Sanyo Cup

BY NIGEL STARMER-SMITH

Put a squad of world-class players from ten different countries on the field with Newcastle, the ebullient champions of England, add in a sunny day at Twickenham and you knew you had the ingredients for a rousing occasion to bring down the curtain on a season of extraordinary but often unpleasant character. It was pleasing, for once, to indulge oneself in some rugby fun – something that the game has left behind in its headlong rush into professionalism.

The 3rd Sanyo Cup match between the World XV, under the guiding hand of Bob Dwyer, and the English Premiership champions displayed talent to whet the appetite of any rugby aficionado. Philippe Sella was captain of the World XV once again on this farewell game in the UK. With him were fellow Frenchmen Stephane Glas, Philippe Bernat-Salles and their Five Nations Championship-winning leader Raphael Ibanez. There were Springboks Pienaar, Hurter and Strauss. Rush of New Zealand lined up alongside Wallabies Waugh and Knox. But perhaps the most appealing story of all was the return to action of the black Springbok wing Chester Williams, the player who had

been so much the symbol of all that was good about the 1995 Rugby World Cup, but whose subsequent knee injuries kept him out of rugby for two years.

It was an assembly certain to provide no mean challenge for the Newcastle outfit, led on this occasion by their departing Scotland international Alan Tait. For once there were no league points, promotion aspirations or championship status at stake – just a cup that was destined to overflow once more with rugby entertainment. But who, one wondered, would steal the show and follow the example of Fijian Waisale Serevi, who had scored a hat-trick of tries in a remarkable individual performance 12 months before.

We did not have long to wait for the answer. Within half an hour, Philippe Bernat-Salles,

Three solid citizens in the World XV front row: from the left, South Africa's Marius Hurter, England's Richard Cockerill and Australia's Cameron Blades.

Philippe Bernat-Salles, the 'Pau Rocket', darts inside on his way to one of his three tries.

the 'Pau Rocket', picked the ball off the deck, cut inside, skinned the defence and sprinted home to complete a personal hat-trick of tries. There was no doubting the magnitude and brilliance of his achievement. The Middlesex 7s apart, I wonder whether Twickenham has ever witnessed its equal. And that was just one course of a rugby feast – 14 tries in all, shared seven apiece.

The World XV had won the Sanyo Cup on both the previous occasions it had been contested, beating Leicester in 1996 and Wasps the following year. Today Newcastle were to have the final say but only after a dramatic turn of events ensured their success. The game served to re-emphasise what in truth we had always known: the importance to Newcastle of their canny half backs, Rob Andrew and Gary Armstrong. Rob had been happy to give two younger understudies a run – Chris Simpson-Daniel at scrum half and the player who was to be an England international fly half before the summer was through, Jonny Wilkinson. Suffice it to say that for the 40 minutes of the first half, Newcastle looked jaded and had been run ragged by the brilliance of Bernat-Salles' hat-trick along with hugely appreciated

tries from Chester Williams (with his first touch of the ball) and Philippe Sella on his farewell. With three conversions by David Knox added, Newcastle trailed 19-31 at half-time.

Enter the Anglo-Scottish pairing at half back; exit the youngsters. Not that the transformation was immediate. Two further World XV tries by Argentinian scrum half Agustin Pichot increased his side's lead to 22 points. However, with their Director of Rugby in place, Newcastle began to control affairs. Ultimately and dramatically they turned the tables, drawing on their other principal assets, team spirit (aka pride) and their abrasive, physical style. The hits got bigger as superior force held sway. Gary Armstrong and Pat Lam added two tries to the two by Tait and one by Nesdale scored in the

The popular Chester Williams returned from long-term injury to score with his first touch of the game.

first half. Wilkinson had converted two of those three first-half tries, and with Rob Andrew kicking three out of three second-half conversions all was set for a grandstand finish. With just three minutes remaining, the scoreline stood at 41-40 to the World XV. The coup de grace was predictable enough, with one of Newcastle's own 'World' players, Va'aiga Tuigamala, all bullocking force and momentum, bursting his way to the line for the winning try, converted by Andrew, for a victory by 47 points to 41.

The second half served to underline just how Newcastle had powered their way to the Allied Dunbar Premiership title and how teamwork, determination and sheer power play can usually overcome the superior footballing skills of a 'pick-up' team of diverse talents. Once again, the Sanyo Cup provided the welcome relief of festival fare at the end of a long, uncomfortable season.

For some individuals the game had a special significance. For the returning Chester Williams, 'It meant a lot to be back in action playing first-class rugby again. Now I can set my sights on making South Africa's 1999 World Cup squad.' For the departing Philippe Sella, 'I think our [World XV's] problem was that we started off too late [kick-

Newcastle scrum half Gary Armstrong whips away another pass. An immensely experienced campaigner, Armstrong led Newcastle's Sanyo revival along with fellow 'evergreen', fly half Rob Andrew.

SKILL, SPEED AND STAMINA.

WE CAN HELP YOU TO IMPROVE

YOUR PERFORMANCE.

off was 3.15] and the weather was too hot! My farewell experience was not a sad occasion. For me, rugby is one life. That is finished and now I have another life. My business interests will take over, and I know now I must stop. I learnt a lot over 17 years. I made a lot of friends around the world – why should I be sad?'

Alan Tait, who was Newcastle captain for the day on his farewell appearance, had this to say: 'I had been running and hiding from Rob [Andrew] for a while because I had not wanted to tell him I was leaving Newcastle, before we had wrapped up the league season. Last night I finally had to come clean – and he gave me the honour of leading the team today. I couldn't believe it. It's been a great time with Newcastle. Rob saved my career from Rugby League, and what with Scotland, the Lions and now all our success with Newcastle it couldn't have gone any better.'

The 1998 Sanyo Cup match was Philippe Sella's farewell match in the UK. François Pienaar leads the Twickenham crowd in saluting a rugby legend.

And Pat Lam, Newcastle's Player of the Season, explained the secrets of Newcastle's success: 'Our success stems from the enthusiasm of Sir John Hall, which has rubbed off on all of us, through the coaching staff and playing squad, and winning has become something of a habit for us. At the outset we received so much criticism for the fact that we were a squad which was made up of players from so many places, but the criticisms made us a stronger unit. I've been in rugby a long time, and team spirit is the key element in champions.'

Inevitably, the celebrations were muted. This day apart, frankly there had been precious little to celebrate this season. Did anyone stop to ask why there were a mere 18,000 or so spectators present at Twickenham (capacity 72,000) to witness a splendid occasion with players of such talent on view? Yet more evidence of the malaise that has afflicted the game. Who said rugby football was thriving?

As if the home season had not been not bad enough, spilling over as it did with acrimony and subterfuge between warring factions, what followed on England's tour to the southern hemisphere brought the game to yet lower depths in this bleakest episode in English rugby history. And if one could partially excuse the humiliation of the senior national team on account of the absence of so many leading players (not forgetting why they were missing), what then of the performance (and similar cricket-score defeats) of the representative England Under 21 side? Suffice it to say that those who have formulated RFU council policy until now (July 1998), as well as the RFU membership that has allowed it to happen, must surely realise that they have effectively surrendered control of the game to a handful of clubs. They should be made accountable for their actions in bringing the game – and England rugby – into disrepute; perhaps even for destroying its very essence.

Meanwhile, and heaven knows what's in store, make a date for some rugby fun at the Sanyo Cup in May 1999.

EUROPE WITHOUT ENGLAND: the 1998-99 Heineken Cup

BY JOHN KENNEDY

South Africa, Saracens and Llanelli will be doing it in 1999, but Bath won't. While the Springboks will defend their world crown and Sarries and the Scarlets their domestic English and Welsh cup titles, Bath will have to hand over their European mantle without even putting up the merest whiff of a fight.

The withdrawal of England's top clubs from the 1998-99 European Cup tournament has left Bath high and dry, the champions counted out and unable to make any sort of defence of the trophy they lifted against all the odds when they sensationally beat Brive 19-18 in Bordeaux back in January. At the time Bath match winner and full back Jon Callard declared, 'They [the competition organisers] have got it spot on. I don't agree with the boycott and it [the competition] just has to continue.'

But sentiments of that sort counted for nothing when it came to the real thing – the power game for control of the club game. After just two seasons, Europe has become a no-go area for the cream of England, their clubs also absent from next season's European Shield. Both Euro-competitions will be the poorer for the protest, while Newcastle, Saracens, Bath and Leicester will miss out on substantial cash bonanzas. However, the party goes on without them, with the 16 best from France, Wales, Scotland, Ireland and Italy doing battle to try and follow Toulouse, Brive and Bath as the cocks of the north.

While France have dominated the second-tier tournament – the Conference, renamed the European Shield – by supplying all the semi-finalists so far, the main event has been far more cosmopolitan, Cardiff, Leicester and Bath going all the way to the showpiece occasions. Nevertheless, the French will yet again be the ones to beat. Their new champions, Stade Français, bring Paris into the venue equation for the first time, with the hotbed down south represented by ever-present Toulouse – invariably many people's pre-tournament favourites – Perpignan, Colomiers and Bègles-Bordeaux. Among the newcomers boosting Toulouse's already star-studded squad is All Black threequarter Lee Stensness, while fellow Kiwi international Eric Rush and Italian scrum half Lucas Martin will be turning out in the blue-and-white colours of Bègles.

Stade Français, bankrolled by wealthy radio-station owner Max Guazzini, have been revitalised. They won the French Club Championship in real style, hammering Perpignan 37-7 in the final after doing much the same to Toulouse in the semi-finals, when the margin of victory was 36 points. With Italian fly-half ace Diego Dominguez pulling the strings – not to mention kicking the points – and new England cap Richard Pool-Jones and French hardman Marc Lievremont packing down together in the back row, they also reached the French Cup final, only for Toulouse to get their revenge.

Colomiers, who clinched the Conference crown last season with a scintillating 43-5 demolition of Agen, may be based just a punt away from their more famous neighbours, Toulouse, but with hooker Marc Dal Maso having arrived from Agen they are intent on emerging from the Toulouse shadow. Current French captain Raphael Ibanez has also been on the move during a frenetic transfer season, troubled Dax losing yet another of their top players as the hooker signed for Perpignan. Fly half Didier Camberabero has also linked up with France's most southerly club as they prepare for the big time.

Swansea, who romped away with the Welsh National League title, will be banking on new skipper and Lions centre powerhouse Scott Gibbs to help them make a real mark on the Euro-scene. Inconsistency has been their downfall in many instances in the past. Meanwhile, battle-hardened Pontypridd – only six points separated them from Brive after three high-profile clashes – have really taken on board the European challenge and certainly deserved the kinder draw this time after being in the same pool as cup finalists Bath and Brive last season. Ebbw Vale will be testing the temperature of the top level for the first time after a debut finish in Wales' top four, while Cardiff, bristling with big names, are desperate to fulfill their undoubted potential.

The Irish challenge is likely to be spearheaded again by Leinster under their Welsh coach Mike Ruddock. The Leicester Tigers and Milan were among their victims last season. Munster, however, have proved an extremely tough nut to crack, in particular on their own patch at Musgrave Park in Cork. Scotland (now fielding just two teams following the amalgamation of Edinburgh and Scottish Borders into the Edinburgh Reivers and Glasgow and Caledonia into Glasgow Caledonia) have been the underachievers so far, although Glasgow did reach last season's quarter-final play-offs.

The demise of Milan as one of Italian rugby's pacesetters has opened the way for Padova to join Treviso in flying the Azzurri flag. Padova, who have probably been more famous for their David Campese connection than anything they have achieved in the past, pushed Treviso all the way in the Italian Cup final before going down 9-3. They could prove a surprise package, while Treviso, with the mighty backing of Benetton, are going from strength to strength.

Pontypridd's Geraint Lewis sprints away to score a breakaway try against Brive during the Welsh side's home leg against the then European champions in the 1997-98 competition.

If the European Cup challenge to the Celts and the Italians is how to stop the French, then it is a double helping of the same in the Shield competition. The talent the French clubs can put out is awesome. The hectic summer transfer merry-go-round stopped spinning on 1 July and ended up with Castres able to parade fly half Thomas Castaignède, All Black Frank Bunce and Irishman Jeremy Davidson, while Brive have been as busy as anyone in the comings-and-goings department. The 1997 European Cup winners – it must be short odds on them adding the Shield to their honours – swooped for Scottish star Gregor Townsend and French international backs Olivier Campan and David Berty. It all makes for mouthwatering stuff, and the crying shame is that the names of players like Archer, Weir, Nicol, Perry, Guscott, Dawson, Johnson, Back, Diprose and Wallace will be among those conspicuous by their absence when talk turns to Euro-matters.

Bath have beaten holders Brive to win the 1997-98 Heineken European Cup. Recreation Ground heroes Victor Ubogu and Adedayo Adebayo are elated; the French players less so.

Choosing Your Franchise:
Do you know what to look for?

THIS INFORMATION IS BASED ON KNOWLEDGE WE HAVE ACCUMULATED ON THE REASONS WHY BUSINESSES PROSPER OR FAIL

DO YOU GET
A HIGH LEVEL OF SUPPORT
AND TRAINING?

ARE YOU ALLOWED
TO TALK TO EXISTING
FRANCHISEES?

ARE THERE FIXED
OPENING HOURS?
DO THEY SUIT YOU?

Choosing the right franchise depends heavily on how well you evaluate potential franchisors. Midland's Franchise Start-Up Pack helps you work out who to sign up with. There's a video, booklet and CD Rom business game – all are full of useful tips and relevant questions for you to ask.

Midland Bank

Member HSBC *Group*

www.midlandbank.com

For your free Start-Up Pack phone **0345 40 41 42** or visit your local branch.

BRITISH
FRANCHISE
ASSOCIATION
AFFILIATE

FR15

ON THE HOME FRONT

THE RECALL OF 99: the reunion of the '74 Lions

BY **NIGEL STARMER-SMITH**

Which was the greatest Lions tour of all? The argument will never be settled and rightly so. First, define the word 'greatest'. I think I can safely suggest that the 1955 Lions tour of South Africa, which began against Northern Transvaal on 22 June and finished with the fourth Test on 24 September, was socially the most successful. With the likes of Tony O'Reilly, Cliff Morgan, Jeff Butterfield, Tom Reid, Robin Roe, Dick Jeeps et al in their number that kind of success was, I guess, inevitable. To be fair, they also drew the Test series two-all. The journeys out and home by sea must have been epic experiences in themselves.

In strictly playing terms many would point to the first-ever Lions Test triumph over the All Blacks in 1971 as the greatest achievement. The triumvirate of John Dawes (captain), Carwyn James (coach) and Doug Smith (manager) guided a legendary assembly of British Isles rugby talent to unprecedented success – a historic two Test to one series victory. This was the golden age of Barry John and Gareth Edwards, Mike Gibson and JPR Williams, McBride and McLauchlan, Gerald Davies, Mervyn Davies and David Duckham.

But only one Lions team travelled unbeaten through a tour, winning 21 matches and drawing just one (the fourth and final Test match), and that was the sequel to 1971 – Willie-John McBride's Lions of 1974 in South Africa. There was an important nucleus remaining from the previous tour – McBride himself (now captain), Edwards, JPR, Gibson, Mervyn Davies, Fergus Slattery, Gordon Brown, Ian McLauchlan, and Sandy Carmichael – to which were added the precocious talents of Andy Irvine, Phil Bennett and JJ Williams, the midfield solidity of Dick Milliken and Ian McGeechan, and forward juggernauts in the shape of Fran Cotton, Roger Uttley and Bobby Windsor.

Once more this was a vintage crop, which cavorted through South Africa in triumph, leaving Springbok rugby in ruins in their wake. Certainly if an ability to win owes as much to opposition limitations as it does to your own strengths, then South Africa certainly helped to smooth the Lions' path. Never has Springbok rugby been at such a low ebb as it was in 1974.

It is impossible for me to draw a comparison between the two rival Lions tours for the title of the greatest: one I saw only in brief film excerpts; the other, in 1974, I witnessed blow by blow from start to finish. Suffice it to say that as an initiation to Lions touring as a 'cub' BBC commentator (working 'blind', so to speak, to film cameras – no such thing as a monitor, or a television picture, in those pre-TV days in South Africa) it was a mind-blowing experience. The onfield success was extraordinary, the style of play so exhilarating, the good humour and fun hard to better, and the intimacy between the playing party and the small media troupe something to cherish. It was never to be the same again. In my experience then, they were undoubtedly the greatest of Lions.

To coincide with the special anniversary of the 1974 Lions, the Recall of 99 has been arranged as a reunion 'tour' in aid of the Wooden Spoon Society, very much on the lines of the reunion of their predecessors in May 1996. So next spring there will be a programme of events throughout the British Isles, centred on Edinburgh, Dublin, Cardiff and London, combining celebration dinners and golf days, culminating in a Gala Dinner at the London Hilton, Park Lane, on Friday 21 May. The players will be there; might I suggest that you might like to *be there,* too?

be there!

*Hunting Lions.
Far right, top: Ian McGeechan on the burst, supported by Phil Bennett and JJ Williams.
Far right, bottom: No. 8 Mervyn Davies takes on the Springboks.
Right: Gordon Brown feeds scrum half Gareth Edwards.*

Far left: The all-conquering '74 Lions. Back row, l-r, CFW Rees, JJ Moloney, SA McKinney, RTE Bergiers, FE Cotton, TP David, GW Evans, WCC Steele, IR McGeechan. Middle row, l-r, RW Windsor, JJ Williams, AGB Old, A Neary, RM Uttley, CW Ralston, AG Ripley, TO Grace, MA Burton, RA Milliken, AR Irvine, P Bennett. Front row, l-r, JPR Williams, TM Davies, J McLauchlan, GO Edwards, AG Thomas (Manager), WJ McBride (Captain), S Millar (Assistant Manager), GL Brown, KW Kennedy, JF Slattery, AB Carmichael.

WAS IT WORTH IT?

BY **JOHN REASON**

Judging by the splendidly peremptory tone of the International Board's letter to the disaster area flatteringly known as the Rugby Football Union (some union!), it has borne in upon the IB that they are now looking down the barrel of the collapse of the game worldwide. The IB would not have written 'These are not options. They are requirements', if it were otherwise.

To some of us – sadly, to all too few of us who write about the game – the only mild surprise is that the members of the International Board are actually prepared to recognise and admit the reality. After all, they pulled the plug with the bit of procedural gerrymandering that managed to avoid a vote on the amateurism requirement that has always been the first commandment of the game.

That they have had a change of heart is more than you can say for that catastrophically inadequate oligarchy of self-perpetuating ostriches trying and failing to pass as the governing body of Rugby Union football in England. Happily, though, the International Board have obviously heard of Mr Micawber. They respect his thunderbolts of common sense. Micawber's first law of economics held that 'Annual income twenty pounds, annual expenditure nineteen nineteen six, result happiness.' His second law stated that 'Annual income twenty pounds, annual expenditure twenty pounds ought and six, result misery.' Mr Micawber did not say what income twenty pounds, expenditure four million pounds would lead to. They are the mathematics of the madhouse and, quite rightly, it never even occurred to him that anybody could be so stupid as to employ them. Or that a so-called governing body could effectively sanction them.

But then, he did not know the sort of people who would be bringing Rugby Union football to its knees at the end of the twentieth century. He would never have believed that small, small men, chronically lacking in common sense, and quite devoid of business knowledge, would preside over an arrangement that would result in the very swift bankruptcy of some of the greatest rugby clubs in England. Even worse, they have actually defended that arrangement and mustered their battalions of rotten boroughs to protect it. Instead of telling the Walter Mittys in their so-called senior clubs that financial mismanagement in international telephone numbers was not an option, they waved the white flag and bleated lamely about 'trying to keep the game together'.

What game? At the rate it is going downhill (in fact it is in free fall), there will not be a game in the United Kingdom in two years time. And England will be to blame. From the beginning, it has shrieked from the heavens that most, though not quite all, of the men buying up England's top clubs were either property developers or asset-strippers, or both. They bought those clubs on the infallible entrepreneurial principle of 'Heads we win; tails you lose'. The game? Oh, sod that!

The fact is that professionalism in club rugby simply is not viable anywhere in the United Kingdom. The top provinces in the southern hemisphere, and only the top provinces, can just about raise enough money to make a case for it, but without national unions having primacy when it comes to contracting players, and control of players' movements, even that would not work. South Africa will discover that later this year when the players' existing contracts expire and it becomes an open market. Already, provinces like Northern Transvaal are committing themselves to expenditure that they cannot possibly afford.

Even for the southern hemisphere – and especially for the United Kingdom and France – shamateurism was far, far better than professionalism. Some years ago, I talked about this with Dr Louis Luyt, the president of the South African Rugby Union. I made an estimate of what François Pienaar was being paid as an amateur. I then said what he would ask for as a professional. Some time later, I saw Dr Luyt again. 'You were right, John,' he said. Grimly. 'Nearly to a penny.'

Yet nowhere has the biter been bit more severely than in Wales. In the free-booting (sorry, fill-booting) days of shamateurism, Llanelli could pay their players out of the proceeds from the car park and were one of the leading clubs in Europe. But when the game went professional, Llanelli went bankrupt. In six months. All the top clubs in Wales except Cardiff are now bankrupt. And if it were not for the millions made by the famous Stan the Pies, and inherited by his son Peter, Cardiff would have been smashed into smaller smithereens than any of them. But even for Peter, whom I met on the Cardiff tour of South Africa in 1967, philanthropy must have a limit.

What is even worse than the financial idiocy is the ruthless exploitation of the bodies of the players. Rugby, with its tackling and scrummaging, is an impact sport, and the full-time training that has come with professionalism has increased fitness levels and body strength to the point where impacts are infinitely more damaging than they were, and there are far more of them. No player will enjoy a 15-year career now. He will be lucky to last five. And he certainly will not enjoy it as he did when the social side of the game was as marvellous as the playing of it. Now the players turn up, play, walk off (or are

Llanelli's famous ground Stradey Park. Financial problems forced the Scarlets to sell it to the Welsh Rugby Union.

Skipper Lawrence Dallaglio, seen here captaining Wasps in the Tetley's Bitter Cup final, was just one of many England players who finished the season carrying injuries.

A huge gap exists between giants and tiddlers in the World Cup, a gap that has widened with professionalism.

carried off), shower, change, get on the bus and go home. Just like professional soccer players.

The unlimited substitution of players has added greatly to the risk of injury. Through the use of substitutes, the tiredness factor is vastly reduced, so the space available for the player on the field has been reduced as well. Also, players are urged to play through injuries for the money and the points. Most of the England team was crippled at the end of last season.

Even when it is at full strength, it would be flattering to call the present England team undistinguished. I never thought I would live to see Scotland, Ireland and Wales reduced to the depths they are at now. England are just the best of a very, very poor bunch. But the beauty of the old Five Nations Championship was that a consideration of that sort simply did not matter. It was the event that mattered and the fun of the biennial calendar. On those terms, the Five Nations Championship made England, Scotland, Ireland, Wales and France completely self-sufficient. That was why the tournament was envied so much by the southern hemisphere.

That this was so was confirmed for me back in 1984, when Australia's Nick Shehadie and New Zealand's Dick Littlejohn came over to London to try to whip up support for the idea of a World Cup. They took me out to dinner in London as a part of that exercise. Nick represented the Australian RU; Dick represented New Zealand.

When they admitted what they were up to, I grinned and said, 'That's carrying coals to Newcastle lads. The World Cup was my idea in the first place.' Great jocularity all round. 'What are we wasting our money for?' laughed Nick. But it was a good evening. At the end of it, I said, 'Come on now. What is this all about?' There was a pause. Then Dick said, 'Go on. Tell him.' Nick leaned forward with his arms on the table. 'We want to reduce the influence of the Four Home Unions,' he said. 'And we want to reduce the status of the Five Nations Championship.'

Well, they have certainly done that. And I have lived to regret what I said about the inevitability of a World Cup – and club leagues, and club cup competitions. The members of the various rugby unions at the time howled with outrage when I wrote these things. 'Over our dead bodies,' they said.

I know now that the game is not well served by these innovations. Also, the gap between the haves and the have-nots of world rugby is so huge that the World Cup ought to be banned by law as a ridiculously unfair and dangerous event – and that gap has been made much, much bigger by professionalism. We have already had scores of more than 100 points. We have already had a quadraplegic spinal injury. What sort of a competition is that?

We are lucky that the American legal profession does not seem to be aware of the enormous possibilities that are now available to them in this country. They could make even more money than the asset-strippers out of the crippling injuries that are being inflicted on our players. But what an appalling indictment of the game!

The so-called agreements negotiated by the Rugby Union with the so-called senior clubs amount to unconditional surrender. Eleven points at issue; eleven white flags. Neville Chamberlain was a Boadicea by comparison. It would not be quite so bad if those spendthrift clubs were doing anything for the game in England or for the national team. But they are not. Just the reverse. As Fran Cotton so rightly said, all they are doing is paying the old-age pensions of southern hemisphere has-beens. That is no good to England. So why should they be given any money at all by the Rugby Union? Better by far to show them the way to the bicycle shed. They would not last six months. A minority at the Rugby Union have seen all this clearly. I am told that the Rugby Union is technically bankrupt. Certainly, Graeme Cattermole, who fills the post once known as treasurer, came very close to admitting as much at the union's recent annual meeting.

No one saw the reality more clearly than did Cliff Brittle. He was twice elected chairman of the RFU, but he was short of political and presentation skills. Worse, the appeasers in the RFU, the men in the pockets of the big clubs, launched a vendetta against Brittle, and managed to raise enough proxy votes from the services, the universities and the students to bring him down. At the annual meeting there was a great furore when it was dicovered that all the Oxford University proxies were signed by the same person. The real clubs rightly sniff at those proxies, which, as I say, they regard as rotten boroughs. But only shareholders are allowed to vote at the annual meetings of most public companies, and I doubt whether any of the proxies raised from the services, the students and the universities would have any legal standing as shareholders, and neither would the members of the Rugby Union themselves.

Not that it matters much now. As the IB seem to have realised, the game is too far gone to be concerned with quibbles. Vernon Pugh is the IB chairman. He it was who manipulated that fateful meeting in Tokyo to avoid a vote on the central issue of professionalism. He knew that if a vote had been taken, the southern hemisphere countries would have been obliged to break away. So there would have been no World Cup in Wales in 1999. Looking at the mess the game is in now, I have to ask: Was it worth it?

International Board chairman Vernon Pugh. 'He it was who manipulated that fateful meeting in Tokyo to avoid a vote on the central issue of professionalism.'

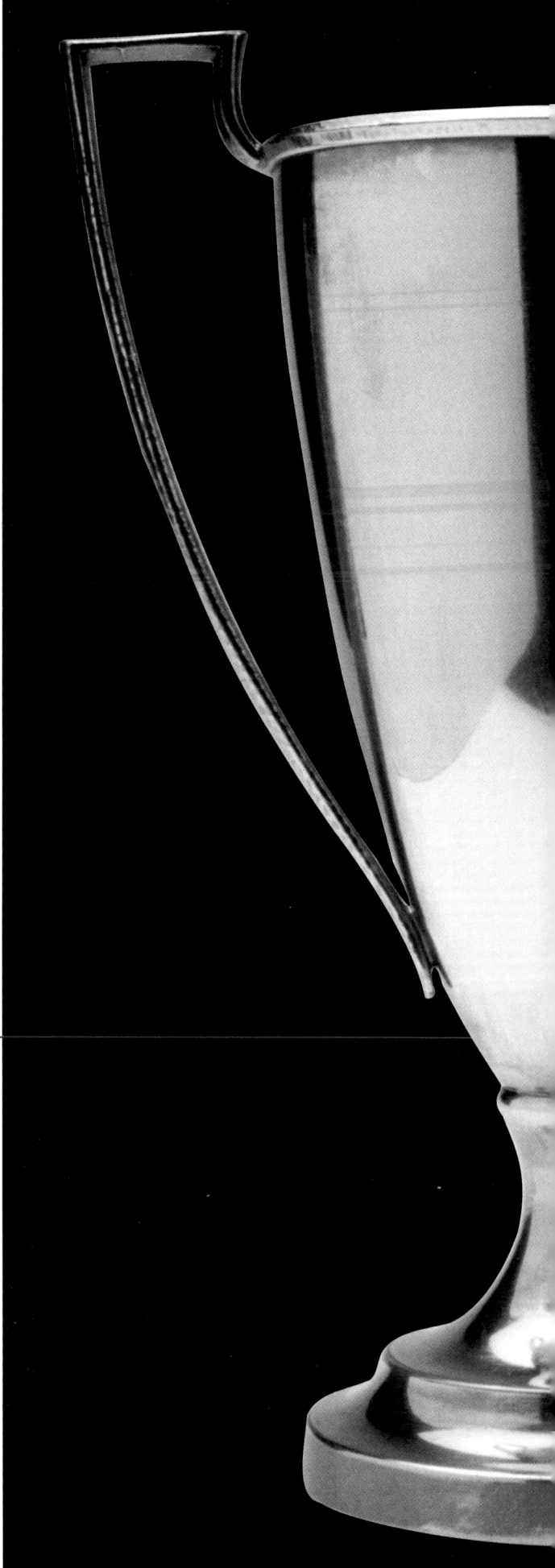

A top team in the field of law.
One step ahead of the game.

winning

Wragge&Co

55 Colmore Row, Birmingham, B3 2AS
Telephone 0121 233 1000 Fax 0121 214 1099
Email post@wragge.com
www.wragge.com

NEC LUSISSE PUDET, SED NON INCEDERE LUDUM

BY **PAUL STEPHENS**

With spin-doctoring elevated to a place alongside the other essential human sciences, it is no wonder that few engaged in this beguiling activity waste an occasion to tell us what a great success Rugby Union in England has become. Yes, there would be the inevitable teething problems once the game embraced professionalism. But these, we were assured so soothingly by those who have been spinning away ever since the ink was applied to the Mayfair Agreement, are all behind us. Anyone dim enough to be taken in by this nugget of 24-carat hokum, would presumably swallow the notion that the maiden voyage of the *Titanic* had not gone quite as well as expected, although the survivors had reached America in good spirits and were apparently none the worse for their experience.

Once it became clear to the members of the Rugby Football Union Council that no meaningful agreement with the leading clubs would ever be reached while Cliff Brittle was acting as their negotiator-in-chief, the RFU sought to settle in haste. This was seen as essential to avoid the potential embarrassment of more big-money sponsors withdrawing their support, as Courage, Save & Prosper, CIS, and Pilkington had done. With a massive capital repayment programme in hand to fund the rebuilding of Twickenham, the RFU needs all the sponsorship cash it can lay its hands on. The last thing any sponsor wants is to be associated with a game engulfed by turmoil and uncertainty.

By ditching Brittle the RFU played straight into the hands of the clubs. They were beginning to despair of ever getting their way while Brittle was striving to effect a settlement on terms more favourable to the RFU than to the clubs. Brittle might have been blessed with the right beliefs, but he possessed the wrong personality. To club investors such as Sir John Hall at Newcastle, Nigel Wray of Saracens and Chrysalis owner Chris Wright, whose interests include Queens Park Rangers and Wasps – men accustomed to getting their own way – Brittle was impossible to do business with. He had to be replaced. It was hardly a surprise when he was.

Having seemingly resolved the Brittle issue, the RFU's next bright idea was to take a more emollient tone and pack their re-jigged negotiating team with doves. Graham Smith, Trevor Richmond and Brian Baister may be well-meaning to their fingertips, with the best interests of the game at heart, but time was not on their side. The club owners, after weeks in which they made little or no progress, were suddenly like children given a free run in the tuck shop. The Mayfair Agreement was cobbled together in the shortest time possible and everything became sweetness and light. With an audible sigh of relief, the RFU announced an end to the bickering and infighting. Common sense had prevailed, and no longer would we hear club owners like Northampton's Keith Barwell declaring that his players would not be released for England matches.

In no time at all, if it hasn't already, this will be seen as just another shaft of moonshine, while far too many in the club game are showing all the signs of being deluded by their own publicity. Having seen off the Barbarians, the club owners won't be content until they have put paid to the British Lions – which they regard as an anachronism – and turn the presentation and organisation of domestic rugby into something which, in more ways than one, will mirror association football. For common sense, you should read hard-headed commercial gain. Some would even go as far as to say greed. Who am I to disagree? Or any of us for that matter? Before we know it, the new game will be stripped of its traditions, and sentiment will become – like the Tour de France cyclists' favourite stimulant, erythropoietin – a banned substance.

You don't believe me? Sound too fanciful, even apocalyptic, does it? As predictions go, it contains more substance than some of the vapid gush we have heard from the clubs, who expect us to believe that everything is as it should be, when the accumulated debt of those in Allied Dunbar Premiership One is in the region of £20 million. Well before the Mayfair Agreement was struck, it was plain that forecasting a rosy future for a professional club game bore as much conviction as predicting the location of the next asteroid strike.

What could be foretold with some certainty was Cliff Brittle's defeat at the Rugby Football Union's Annual General Meeting at Birmingham in July. Having twice defeated the RFU's chosen candidate for the post of chairman of the board of management, there was to be no third time for Brittle or comfort for his closest supporter, Fran Cotton. Brittle and Cotton now have to decide whether to proceed by challenging the competence of the RFU through demanding a vote of no confidence at a Special General Meeting. With the reputation of the RFU at an all-time low after England's disastrous tour to the southern hemisphere, there is little to be gained by further blood-letting, and it is probably best to allow the new chairman, Brian Baister, to settle in to what is an almost impossibly demanding job before settling the RFU's differences with the clubs.

Baister's first task is to prevent the RFU ceding any more ground to the club owners. And secondly to have no truck with those who want the RFU to bail them out when they get into financial difficulties entirely of their own making. We would be justified in thinking Baister may succeed where Brittle failed if we could be sure he had learned a lesson from his predecessor about the necessity of getting the media on his side. Whether by instinct, or because he lacked the innate confidence to deal with the hack pack, Brittle never came to terms with those who make their living by writing and talking about the game. He was almost paranoid about meeting the press. Consequently, he rarely grasped the opportunity to get his views across to the media, leaving those keen to exploit any new divisions between the clubs and the RFU to make up their own minds about how blame should be apportioned.

By the afternoon of the AGM, the leading rugby writers had – almost to a man – deserted Brittle, and he was left to a fate of his own construction. Brittle was not at all a prophet without honour, but he was almost certainly one without a friend. In the countdown to Cliff Brittle being voted out of office, almost all of rugby's ills were blamed on him. Ludicrous and unfair that may have been, but unfairness, rampant cupidity, and the threat to the financial wellbeing of club rugby are just three of the issues facing Baister as he confronts the problems of mismanagement and the self-aggrandisement of some owners – problems which have contributed so disastrously to a game dangerously destabilised at the top.

While Brittle is the fall guy in this sorry and undistinguished passage of English rugby's history, the media themselves have to take some of the blame, as they fell for the hyperbole that passed for fact in a shameful episode of misinformation. There is today

Ciff Brittle, former chairman of the RFU Executive Committee, never managed to get the media on his side. Will his replacement, Brian Baister, be more successful in this respect?

almost as much hype in club rugby as there is in Formula One motor racing. Hardly a morning went by towards the end of last season, without our being able to read that club rugby had not only achieved new heights of excellence, but that record crowds were ample testimony to the game's burgeoning wealth and health. It is, of course, a preposterous deception. No one denies that the modern game is faster and more skilful, or that the players are fitter, although it must be said that the motor for many of these changes has been fuelled by the overseas players – none of whom are qualified to play for England. And you can be sure there will be plenty more where they have come from.

At Saracens – who when they played Newcastle in front of 19,764 had the biggest league gate of the season – much of the success could be put down to the influence of Philippe Sella of France, Australia's Michael Lynagh and former Springbok skipper François Pienaar. For Wasps, though, who were champions the previous year, crowds at Loftus Road dwindled to an average of 5,834 – a drop of 1.9 per cent. But numbers reveal only a part of the problem. Sure, for the most part, gates are up. And so they should be, given the amount of free tickets and discounting that is an essential component in today's marketing. And yet, by our willingness to be seduced by the ballyhoo, we appear to be oblivious to the damage done by many of the changes that have been made, without any apparent thought for the consequences or, in some cases, without the consent of the membership. It is as if we know the price of everything and the value of nothing.

By embracing many of the elements of soccer, rugby is a short step away from discarding its unique value system. The everlasting friendships, the gloriously colourful social mix and proud traditions will soon become little more than misty memories if we

aren't very careful. Already there are signs that club rugby is injudiciously keen to ape professional football. The growth in the number of security personnel at grounds and the relative inaccessibility of players after matches are but two instances of a change in rugby's culture. With a growing number of clubs opting to play in football stadia, the process of change will accelerate, and nothing the RFU can do will interrupt these unwelcome developments – at least not until sanity prevails. And that time may not be too far away, even if the journey has been almost unbearably painful, and the casualty rate unacceptably high.

Saracens won the cup and came second in the Premiership last season. Much of their success could be put down to the influence of overseas players such as Philippe Sella (right), Michael Lynagh and François Pienaar.

In the Allied Dunbar Premiership – where self-interest and overspending foster a continuing atmosphere of instability – if the clubs are to haul themselves back from the precipice, they must first acquire something instructive from what happened at Coundon Road and The Reddings. There, for Coventry and Moseley, receivership was the only option to end the profligacy. If the alarm bells ringing at those famous old grounds don't signal a warning, then what has happened to Bristol surely must.

For Bristol, once one of England's grandest clubs, their slide towards penury is a sorry tale. By adding complacency to overspending and incompetence, the management at the

Coventry are just one of a number of once mighty clubs that have called in the receivers.

Memorial Ground had mixed a combustible cocktail of deficiency, which ultimately became unaffordable. Their millionaire chairman, Arthur Holmes, his loans to the club secured by a charge on a piece of land the club owned, retrieved most of his money, though little of his reputation. Other smaller investors weren't so fortunate.

Those who trumpet the success of the game as measured by record attendances may care to reflect on last season's gates at Bristol and Richmond. They each averaged 3600. Richmond's reaction to this heady upturn in their fortunes has been to move down the M4 to a soccer stadium in Reading, where they can accommodate bigger crowds. Not many years ago, Bristol would expect 3000 for a United XV game; more when they were playing the second teams from Gloucester, Cardiff or Newport.

On the day the receivers arrived at Bristol and he left office in tears, Arthur Holmes had a warning for the future of the game: 'Rugby will never be like soccer. It doesn't have the same appeal.' Holmes should know. He gave his blessing to the ground-sharing deal the rugby club struck with Bristol Rovers.

Bristol have since been struck down by their own folly. As they, Coventry and Moseley try to rescue something from their ineptitude, they may like to consider the words of Horace as a motto for a new club crest or programme cover: *Nec lusisse pudet, sed non incedere ludum* – Not in committing but by prolonging acts of folly is the shame.

Above: Arthur Holmes, the former chairman of Bristol. 'Rugby will never be like soccer. It doesn't have the same appeal,' he said.

The average gate at Bristol's Memorial Ground last season was 3600. Not many years ago the club could have expected something approaching that for a visit by Gloucester's Second XV.

Property Consultants

Leading the Field
Throughout the Midlands

16 Warwick Row
Coventry CV1 1EJ
Tel: 01203 555 180
Fax: 01203 223 434

NICE STADIUM, SHAME ABOUT THE TEAM

BY **EDDIE BUTLER**

Just as New Zealand once had the moa bird and Russia had a tsar, so Wales once had a passion for rugby. But no more, it appears. Having spluttered for the better part of the past two decades, the fires were finally put out by a single scoreline: South Africa 96, Wales 13. The passion for rugby has gone the way of the moa and the Romanovs: it is extinct, executed.

Perhaps it should come as no surprise that rugby in Wales lies cold on the slab. After all, the game was never designed to be played in such a place, or at least not beyond the public schools of Llandovery, Brecon and Monmouth. The few civilised chaps in the land might be tolerated, but the rest were savages. Unfortunately for the founding fathers in England, rugby fever in Wales was ignited by the fires of the steam trains of the nineteenth century that brought a labour force from Gloucestershire and Somerset to industrial valleys and ports. Liverpool and Manchester carried association football to North Wales; the West Country of England brought rugby football to the south. If ever there had been a north-south railway network, and not just these east-west lines, Gareth Edwards would have been the heart-throb of Ninian – not the Arms – Park; of Cardiff City AFC – not Cardiff RFC.

The early predecessors of the Great One were drawn immediately to rugby's twin attractions of creativity and violence. Imagination and nimble feet walked the same fields as thugs, ref-baters and pitch-invaders by the thousand. The early years of the twentieth century were a golden period of brilliance and brutality, the participants and the followers inspired by the simple logic that this was the best – possibly the only – way of putting one over the English. Welsh nationalism in the south always had this outlet in rugby. It was only in the north, in Gwynedd and on Anglesey, that a bomb meant more than an up-and-under at Twickenham.

An artist's impression of the new stadium at Cardiff. Will it be it a mausoleum to rival the Pyramids, or a monument to the future?

Wales still in the driving seat, but not for much longer. Bob Norster drives Wales forward during the 1987 World Cup quarter-final, which Wales won 16-3.

If the attractions came as a pair, so did the reasons for decline. For nearly 100 years everything seemed fine and rosy. And nothing was finer than the decade of the 1970s, when Wales humbled England all too often. Even in the less successful 1980s, Wales still had the upper hand, and the record of England's inability to win at Cardiff after 1963 stretched way beyond 20 years. (Slight hiccough in 1983 when there was a draw. Personally, I blame the captain.)

But then, in 1987, after England had been knocked out of the first World Cup by Wales in the quarter-finals, somebody at Twickenham took a decision. Enough was enough. It was time for England to begin to take rugby seriously. And so began the era of Geoff Cooke, Roger Uttley and Will Carling – manager, coach and captain. England were not pretty, but they were heavyweight and they started to explore a logic of their own, which told them that England has nearly 20 times the population of Wales. The logic of passion met the logic of statistics, and Wales have struggled ever since.

Even worse was to come. The game went professional. Millions now refer not only to playing numbers but to the money needed to keep the new game going. New Zealand have proved that you don't need the population of China to continue to play rather well, but they enjoy advantages at the bottom end of the southern oceans not available to Wales, who are locked to England like some talented but impoverished cousin kept in the west wing in case he embarrasses the family by telling foul jokes during brandy and cigars. New Zealand have a national commercial infrastructure, for example, which allows their game to prosper. They are backed by a national airline and a pan-national television deal, and it is impossible not to know that they have a multinational brewery, Steinlager, behind them, if not on top of them.

There is a television company in Wales, called S4C (Sianel Pedwar Cymru), which has all the clout of Swindon Hospital Radio. And, er, that's about it. There are a lot of ex-mines and a lot of closed factories. Of course, there are lots of Japanese plants and Korean enterprises – but it was just Wales' luck that the day they took their marketing plans and sponsorship opportunities to all these investors from Southeast Asia was the very day the Tiger economies all went into recession.

And so, the spirit of rugby is flagging. In fact, it's even worse than that. The last bits with any feeling have been seized by the pincers of irony. Welsh rugby is dying, so what do they go and do? They go and knock down the Arms Park and engage in a race against time to build a stadium that will make Ceaucescu's palace in Bucharest look like Mrs Eirlys Evans' end-of-terrace in Upper Row, Garndiffaith. A stadium fit for the World Cup final of 1999? More like a mausoleum to rival the Pyramids.

Let's say it once and for all. Welsh rugby is dead. Or is it? Somewhere amid the brutality of modern professionalism is stirring the notion that money isn't everything, that old values count for more than neon marketability. There is still a spirit, dormant but alive. Nobody, but nobody, has mastered the forces of commercial rugby, and those that are currently ahead of the game may soon be in for a rude awakening. Those that are struggling may emerge all the stronger for having been squeezed out of the bear pit.

It may take years – perhaps many years – to assemble the package that guarantees prosperity for a special corner of the rugby world, but rugby will not perish in Wales. The old attractions are still more vibrant than the new realities. The new stadium is not so much a mausoleum, but a monument to the future, a statement of confidence. Somewhere deep in the bush of the upper Swansea Valley the tracks of a moa bird lead to a small cottage where a family of Romanovs live, biding their time.

The shape of things to come? New Zealander Graham Henry, the new Wales coach, in conference with his successful former charges, Auckland. Can Henry help re-ignite the Welsh passion for the game?

SUMMER OF SHAME

WHITEWASH: a national disaster

BY IAN ROBERTSON

The scoreboard says it all: a record 76-0 defeat for England at the hands of Australia. An outrageous itinerary and a lack of cover for absent top players left England at the mercy of the top southern hemisphere sides.

Long before England flew to Brisbane in the last week of May, everyone involved with the tour knew only too well they were embarking on mission impossible. It hardly came as a surprise that England failed to win any of the seven matches they played. There were several contributory factors to their ultimate downfall, but far and away their biggest single problem was the itinerary. The members of the RFU committee who negotiated, then signed up to this deal should either resign or at the very least give a written guarantee that they will never again subject England to such a horrendous tour.

It defies belief that one of the Five Nations sides should contemplate flying to the other side of the world to play Australia after a flight of over 20 hours and a time difference of 9 hours, then fly another 1000 miles to New Zealand with an 11-hour time difference from the UK. If that was not bad enough, the squad then flew 28 hours via Hong Kong to play in South Africa, which is 10 hours behind New Zealand. The leading spread-betting company in Europe – Sporting Index – were no fools when they produced rather ungenerous odds when I enquired about the possibility of England rewriting the record books with three losses in four weeks to Australia, New Zealand and South Africa by record scores.

Apart from the insane fixture list, which meant England had shot themselves in both feet and been knee-capped as well, the difficulties for the England coach, Clive Woodward, were further exacerbated by the withdrawal for a variety of reasons of a large number of his top players. Of the best 35 players in England, about half made themselves unavailable. Some just did not fancy participating in such a crazy tour. A few were genuinely injured. A few others opted out with injuries that did not stop them playing the last four weeks of the domestic season for their clubs but, surprisingly, rendered them unavailable for England. Clive Woodward and his assistant, John Mitchell, found it hard to disguise their displeasure at having such a huge number of first-choice selections drop out, but that was nothing to the disgust and contempt felt by the Australian and New Zealand rugby authorities.

It was always likely that England would be capable of cobbling together a decent pack, and that did indeed prove to be the case, but the back division was undeniably lightweight. Of his first-choice back division for the Five Nations, Clive Woodward landed in the southern hemisphere without half backs Paul Grayson and Kyran Bracken, centres Jeremy Guscott, Will Greenwood and Phil de Glanville and wing threequarter David Rees. He had hoped some of the young, promising, uncapped players would come through and make a real impact on the tour, but, in the main, he was to be disappointed. Indeed by the time of the first Test against the All Blacks he had already determined that three of the centres he had brought on the trip – Steve Ravenscroft, Stuart Potter and Jos Baxendell – were not up to the task. As far as backs were concerned, as part of the build-up to the 1999 World Cup, this tour did not have a great deal of relevance apart from the negative benefit of ruling a lot of players out of contention.

One of England's tormentors at Brisbane, Steve Larkham, struggles to give Danny Grewcock the slip.

The opening Test match against Australia in Brisbane could scarcely have gone worse. In 127 years of international rugby England had never previously conceded more than 45 points in an international. The defeat in Brisbane by 76 points to nil was not only the biggest loss ever but the margin was more than double the previous record. Although it turned in to the ultimate nightmare scenario, half an hour into the game it was impossible to anticipate the humiliation that was to follow. With ten minutes of the first half left, the Wallabies led 6-0, courtesy of two penalties from Matt Burke. It should really have been 6-6 at that stage, but Jonny Wilkinson had missed two kicks at goal. Then the Australians suddenly moved up a gear and turned pressure into points with a vengeance. In the space of ten minutes they destroyed England with four tries from Toutai Kefu, Steve Larkham, Tim Horan and Ben Tune. Burke added two conversions to his three penalties to give Australia a lead of 33-0. England defended well for the first quarter of an hour of the second half, but then Larkham got his second try and the floodgates opened. In the last 20 minutes of this one-sided match, the Wallabies ran in six more tries. The scorers were Burke, Tune with his second and third scores, George Gregan, Larkham with his third and Horan with his second. Burke and Larkham each added two conversions.

England were outscored by 11 tries to nil. Never has an English international side been so completely outplayed and so embarrassingly overwhelmed. It was a disastrous day for English rugby and a stark reminder of the many problems that now confront England. It is too simplistic to blame everything on a weak, depleted, inexperienced side. The pack was not that far from full strength apart from a couple of the back-row forwards. The other reasons have to be addressed as well. In the whole of 1998, the All Blacks will play only seven Tests, and their top international players will play only 30 matches, including those seven Tests. Contrast that with England. In the nine months of the English season up to the Springbok Test in Cape Town, the leading English players have had the opportunity to play in 12 Test matches and more than 30 club matches. The RFU and the clubs must both cut back their demands on the players.

As the party flew from Brisbane to Auckland they knew it was not going to get any easier in New Zealand. However, they did fare a great deal better the following Saturday when they lost only 18-10 to New Zealand 'A' in Hamilton. A mixture of driving rain and a howling wind made the outcome a lottery, and England showed a lot more determination and commitment than they did in Brisbane. Loose forwards Steve Ojomoh and Ben Clarke were outstanding.

The midweek match before the first Test took place at Invercargill, and it produced another high-scoring defeat for England – to the New Zealand Academy by 50 points to 32. Once again the pack played quite well, but the backs were outclassed. Half an hour into the game it was 14-14, but England conceded two tries before half-time to turn round 28-17 behind. They fought back bravely in the second half to cut the deficit to 38-32 with ten minutes remaining, but two late tries from the home side gave the New Zealand Academy a comfortable win.

For the Test in Dunedin the selectors made six changes to the side that played in Brisbane. Up front the whole back row was replaced. Ben Sturnham, Tony Diprose and Richard Pool-Jones made way for Ben Clarke, Steve Ojomoh and Pat Sanderson. Matt Dawson returned at scrum half after injury, with Matt Perry switching from centre to full back, Tim Stimpson moving from full back to the wing and Nick Beal and Josh Lewsey coming in to the side as the new centre pairing.

England faced a new-look All Blacks side without Sean Fitzpatrick, Zinzan Brooke and Frank Bunce, who had all retired, and scrum half Justin Marshall, who was injured. Curiously enough, after half an hour, just as at Brisbane, England trailed by only six

Danny Grewcock's dismissal for kicking All Black hooker Anton Oliver altered the course of the first Test at Dunedin. Until Grewcock was sent off, England were still in the game. Reduced to 14 men, they fell apart.

points. Andrew Mehrtens had kicked three penalties for New Zealand while Tim Stimpson had landed one for England. Then the match changed dramatically as a result of one incident. A scrum near the England posts collapsed, and as the players regained their feet, the referee, Wayne Erickson of Australia, gave a long blast on his whistle and sent off Danny Grewcock for kicking the All Blacks hooker, Anton Oliver, on the head. Although there was no video evidence, the tribunal accepted the referee's report and suspended Grewcock for five weeks. Amazingly, the All Black lock Ian Jones, who was cited by the match commissioner for trampling on Graham Rowntree's head at a ruck, was cleared of any offence and was duly selected for the second Test in Auckland.

With only 14 men, England suddenly, and not surprisingly, fell apart, and the match ended as a contest. In the five minutes that followed the sending-off, New Zealand scored three tries through Christian Cullen (two) and Jonah Lomu. Richard Cockerill burst through to score a try for England to leave the All Blacks 26-8 ahead at the interval.

In the first 20 minutes of the second half New Zealand exended their lead to 57-8, with five more tries from Taine Randell (two), Jeff Wilson (two) and Josh Kronfeld. With ten minutes left, England launched a spirited fightback, with two tries from Matt Dawson and Tom Beim, both converted by Stimpson to leave England trailing 57-22. Right at the end Mark Mayerhofler scored New Zealand's ninth try, and Mehrtens added his fifth conversion to give the All Blacks their biggest-ever victory over England and their highest-ever score against any of the major International Board countries.

If England were overwhelmed in the Test at Dunedin, they were taken apart three days later by the New Zealand Maori team at Rotorua. It would be a kindness to England to simply draw a veil over this, because it was without question the worst shambles I can recall being perpetrated by an England side in the 1990s. They were trounced 62-14 and outscored nine tries to two by a team that contained only one All Black (Adrian Cashmore) and was made up largely of unknown players.

It all pointed to an extremely difficult afternoon at Eden Park in Auckland for the second Test on the Saturday, but to huge relief all round the squad at last came close to fulfilling their limited potential. They played their best rugby of the tour to keep the defeat to almost respectable proportions. It would be foolish to pretend that this 40 points to 10 defeat was actually a good result for English rugby, because it patently wasn't. To put it in context, it was the third-biggest losing margin in an international in the whole of England's 127-year history; the two biggest had come in the previous two Tests in Brisbane and Dunedin.

Nevertheless, the All Blacks were made to work hard for this victory and they looked relatively ordinary for most of the first half. For the first time on the tour the English players were totally focused and completely committed. They not only offered really spirited resistance but were in control of the game for the last 20 minutes of the first half. The English forwards got on top and by winning the majority of possession they kept their side camped in New Zealand territory.

Even so, England trailed 14-0 after a quarter of an hour to tries from Jeff Wilson and Mark Mayerhofler, both of which were converted by Andrew Mehrtens, but they hit back with an excellent try by Matt Dawson ten minutes before the interval. Dawson added the conversion and kicked a penalty early in the second half to cut the deficit to 14-10. It was at this point, though, that the All Blacks hit top form. They ran in four tries through Jeff Wilson, Joeli Vidiri, Isotola Maka and Taine Randell, three of which were converted by Carlos Spencer, to run out convincing and comfortable winners.

On the Sunday the whole circus moved on from Australasia to Cape Town, courtesy of 26 hours in the air with Cathay Pacific. While everyone would accept that Cathay Pacific is one of the world's greatest airlines, it has to be said that a journey of 25 hours flying time covering more than 13,000 miles with a time difference between New Zealand and South Africa of ten hours and a recovery period of just five full days is not the perfect preparation for a Test against the current world champions.

As fate would have it – or perhaps it would be more apposite to say as luck would have it – the weather came to England's aid. The heavens had opened in Western Province the previous week and it rained every day of the week the England party were in Cape Town. By the Saturday the pitch at Newlands had water lying on it and inevitably it turned into a quagmire within minutes of the kick-off. It rained throughout the match, and in monsoon conditions with a slippery ball it was impossible to play decent rugby. It was tailor made for a major English defensive effort – the perfect scenario for a damage-limitation exercise. England did not disappoint.

FACING THE FUTURE WITH NOKIA.

Nokia Telecommunications is at the forefront of tomorrow's technology, developing the solutions to meet the needs of the next generation.

Nokia believes in encouraging achievement, and has built its business on respecting and caring for people, whether customers or suppliers, staff or friends. In our own way we each help to build a better future for everyone, and as part of this Nokia is happy to support the work of The Wooden Spoon.

NOKIA
CONNECTING PEOPLE

Nokia Telecommunications Ltd, Lancaster House, Lancaster Way, Ermine Business Park, Huntingdon, Cambs PE18 6XU, U.K.
Telephone +1480 434444 Fax +1480 435111

Once again the forwards played out of their skins and were outstanding in containing the mighty Springbok pack. The English backs yet again offered nothing in attack worth a light, but they tackled and covered for 80 minutes and ensured the Springbok backs were never able to establish any rhythm or gain any initiative. There were only two lapses. Joost van der Westhuizen charged down an attempted clearing kick on the English 22-metre line and kicked ahead to score the first try midway through the first half. Just before half-time South Africa struck again, when they launched an attack from broken play for Stefan Terblanche to score in the corner. Percy Montgomery added one conversion and kicked two second-half penalties to complete the scoring.

It was an appalling game of rugby played in appalling conditions. It would have taken a very good team to rise above the conditions. On this count South Africa failed badly; England comprehensively. Considering the previous five weeks, though, a defeat of 18-0

was almost acceptable to England. On a dry day it would have been very much worse. It was in this disappointing way that the tour from hell ended.

The record of played seven, lost seven tells its own story. But the England coach Clive Woodward said from the outset that the most important issue was to use the tour to find the best England squad for the World Cup in October 1999. To that end, the tour served a useful purpose. Two backs were outstanding – full back Matt Perry and scrum half Matt Dawson. As an added bonus Dawson developed into an excellent captain. In adversity their skills and character shone through and they will both be key members of the England squad for the next few years.

There were also useful pointers to the future among the forwards. Graham Rowntree, Richard Cockerill and Phil Vickery established themselves as the Test front row. With Kevin Yates and Mark Regan in the wings, England have no problems in this area. Similarly, there is strength in depth at lock. Garath Archer and Danny Grewcock will probably start off as the top locks, but apart from Martin Johnson two new names have emerged. Dave Sims proved his worth, and his Gloucester colleague Rob Fidler showed huge potential. Blooded in a season of games for England 'A', he had no difficulty stepping in to the full international arena and he acquitted himself really well against both New Zealand and South Africa.

In the back row it was good to see Ben Clarke recapture his very best form and he will surely be a regular member of the England squad through to the World Cup. Tony Diprose also had a good tour and Pat Sanderson filled in well at open-side flanker, although he will not have overtaken Richard Hill or Neil Back.

Some lessons were learned for the future, and the tour did help Clive Woodward sort out the wheat from the chaff. But more than anything, Woodward had proof, if proof were necessary, that this was the most ridiculous tour in the history of English rugby. Such an outrageous itinerary must never be arranged again.

Matt Perry takes on the South Africans at Cape Town. Perry, along with namesake and captain Matt Dawson, was one of England's back-line successes Down Under.

TOURS TO SOUTH AFRICA

BY **DAN RETIEF**

*Ireland forwards
Malcom O'Kelly (left)
and Trevor Brennan in
the thick of things
against South Africa.
O'Kelly gave a good
account of himself in
the first Test at
Bloemfontein.*

They came, they saw and they made headlines. The Irish for fighting, the Welsh for holding on to deny South Africa a century, and the English for changing hotels. They did not conquer. In fact, the representatives of three of the home unions played 12 games on their southern African safari and they won just two. Ireland won them both, but against teams who would be rated last and ninth of South Africa's 14 provinces. The four internationals were all lost and – but for Ireland's gaining a grudging admiration for their misplaced bellicosity – the tourists did little that was admirable or competitive. The Irish hung in for 55 minutes in the first Test in Bloemfontein to trail by only five points, but there was never an inkling that any of the three might actually beat the Springboks.

The Irish were the first to arrive, seemingly to the constant refrain of their World Cup song 'Ireland's Call', and were backed by an ever more jolly group of supporters as the Rand slipped to 10 to 1 against the punt. Paddy Johns' men managed a victory at Boland's picturesque ground in Wellington, but made the mistake of overestimating both their own performance and that of a substandard home team. Their dirt-trackers copped it in George; a refereeing error robbed them of a possible win as they packed a line out

with back-line players against Western Province at a sodden Newlands; and then the midweek team were taken apart 52-13 by resurgent former Springbok coach André Markgraaff's impressive Griqualand West in Kimberley.

It must have been round about this time that the Irish decided that if they could not cope with the big, quick, counterattacking backs that are a side product of the Super-12 they would adopt tactics that would make it hard for the Springboks to get into stride at all. South Africa had been forced to pick a new young fly half in Gaffie Du Toit for the first Test in Bloemfontein in place of an injured Henry Honiball, and Johns, as befits a captain, took it upon himself to flatten the youngster with a late charge moments after he'd caught, and kicked, the first ball ever passed to him in a Test match. A few minutes later Du Toit was down again, this time bleeding from a head wound. It was probably at this juncture that control of the temper of the game began to slip away from referee Ed Morrison and in the 30th minute the acrimony was set in stone when Keith Wood felled Gary Teichmann on the side of a maul and well away from the ball.

Irish stand-off Eric Elwood makes a break for it. His goal-kicking and Justin Bishop's try on debut helped keep Ireland in touch at Bloemfontein until Stefan Terblanche and Mark Andrews finally put the Springboks in the safety zone.

With the Irish forwards giving a good account of themselves – especially lock Malcolm O'Kelly and tight-head prop Paul Wallace – it required a stunning debut performance from Stefan Terblanche to carry the Boks in to the safety zone. The youngster from Boland had shot to prominence after being drafted into the Natal Sharks for the Super-12 and took the field in the No. 14 jersey of South Africa's cap record holder James Small – albeit a white Springbok jersey in deference to the emerald of Ireland. Terblanche scored four tries – three of which were outstanding individual efforts requiring pace, strength and grit – to match, on debut, the individual Springbok try-scoring record jointly held by Chester Williams and Pieter Rossouw.

Having convinced themselves that it would be suicidal to leave any loose ball lying around for the dangerous Springbok counterattackers, the Irish did themselves, and their brave pack, a disservice by refusing to try anything expansive. Instead of trying to win, Ireland seemed set on containing the score and thus wasted an opportunity to at least try to come to terms with the high-paced, high-retention game developing in the southern hemisphere. They also failed to grasp that in the possession stakes they had fared pretty well, and instead of resolving to do more with the ball in Pretoria they went into the second Test with much the same attitude.

Sadly, attitudes in the Springbok camp did change. Video replays of the first Test – especially the clash between Wood and Teichmann – stoked the fires, as did rumours emanating from the Irish camp that Johns, Wood and the rest did not think the Boks were all that tough. It's the oldest trick in the book – denigrating the opposition – but the

Springboks took it hook, line and sinker and completely forgot all coach Nick Mallett's admonishments about the need for discipline. The air of animosity was not helped by referee Joel Dumé's theatrical style and his failure to take a strong hand. When, in the fifth minute, the Springboks were denied what would have been a stupendous try from the halfway line for flanker André Venter – because of an alleged offence by Adrian Garvey that the prop adamantly denies ('I *sink* there was a punch,' the ref was heard to say) – you could almost sense the impending explosion.

Joost van der Westhuizen provided it with a disgraceful kick aimed at O'Kelly as the young lock tried to stop the ball from emerging from a maul. The Springbok scrum half, who scored the first try of the match just five minutes later, was yellow-carded, but in fact he was extremely fortunate not to have been sent off. Although the Boks went on to score five tries to nil in a 33-0 victory, both teams shamed themselves, and one trusts every effort will be made to avoid a 'rematch' when the teams meet again at Landsdowne Road in November.

A much-weakened Welsh team were already in the country on a concurrent tour and while their results were equally disappointing, a more adventurous brand of play and a strong fightback against Natal suggested they, at least, had come to play rugby. The Welsh were not expected to actually beat the Boks in Pretoria, but no one could have predicted the massacre that took place at Loftus Versveld –– a ground where, ironically, great Welshmen such as Bobby Windsor, Mervyn Davies, Gareth Edwards, Phil Bennett, JJ Williams and JPR Williams had, with the British Lions in 1974, played a key role in one of South Africa's most humiliating defeats.

Wales saw plenty of Percy Montgomery in their nightmare at Loftus Verfeld. He picked up two tries, nine conversions and a penalty to carry away 31 points from the game – a Bok individual record.

The Springboks did not score a try until the seventh minute. They led 31-6 at half-time. And then the floodgates opened as they ran in 11 tries to score 65 points in the second half and tot up a record score of 96-13, Arwel Thomas having the dubious pleasure of having scored all his team's points. The Welsh ended up providing South Africa with a string of records: highest total, biggest margin, most tries, and the individual scoring record to Bok full back Percy Montgomery, whose two tries, nine conversions and a single penalty gave him a new mark of 31 points.

Worse still, all the Tests were a flop at the gate. High ticket prices might have been a contributing factor, but negative publicity surrounding the withdrawal of high-profile players coupled to poor performances in the build-ups to the Tests certainly caused the public to lose interest. The Blue Bulls Rugby Union (formerly Northern Transvaal) were particularly hard hit. The South African Rugby Union has a system whereby a union has to pay a substantial fee for staging an international, and the men from Pretoria had gambled on a windfall by not only being host to Ireland but also taking over the Welsh Test from struggling Eastern Province.

Instead they showed heavy losses, and afterwards officials indicated they would not again be bidding for Tests featuring weak teams from the home unions. The experience of the Blue Bulls is likely to impact on the decisions of other unions, and the likelihood exists that SARFU will struggle to find provinces willing to host weakened teams from the north – especially when crowds for the Super-12 are substantially bigger and the rugby is markedly more competitive and exciting. Indeed, the mood of dissatisfaction was such that some officials were suggesting that only tours by the British Lions would be acceptable, while the SANZAR nations (South Africa, New Zealand and Australia) were already taking steps to forge closer ties with Argentina, Western Samoa, Tonga and Fiji and investigating means to accelerate the growth of the game in the United States.

After Ireland and Wales, England arrived on what even South African fans agreed was a suicide mission. Having seen the debilitating effect of intercontinental travel on South African teams during the Super-12, there was never any doubt that England would struggle after being pummelled by Australia and New Zealand and then having to make their torturous way from Auckland, via Sydney, Perth and Johannesburg, to Cape Town.

In fact, it might well have been a touch of jet-lag-induced dementia that caused England coach Clive Woodward to suddenly decide to change hotels on the day before the match. England were booked, at their own request, into the Newlands Hotel, just up the road from the ground, which is the traditional Cape Town home of touring teams. The real reason for the change – the fact that the Springboks were in the five-star Cape Sun, the presence of the SA Under 21 team in the Newlands, or pressure from the England wives – will probably never be known, but Woodward uprooted his squad and booked them into the famous and gracious old Mount Nelson at eight times the price! So sudden was Woodward's decision that his assistant, New Zealander John Mitchell, arrived back at the Newlands to find the team departed and no sign of where they gone.

As it turned out, the weather turned nasty, and the bog that passes for an international playing field in midwinter at Newlands tended to level things up a bit. The Springboks had become surprisingly nervous in the build-up and they went into the game determined to take no risks. England were even more sterile (if that's the word given the muddy conditions!) and the upshot was that the Springboks scored two tries to nil and won a dull game 18-0. There was not much to write home about, but Springbok coach Nick Mallett took some pleasure out of the fact that England had not carried the ball into his team's 22-metre area on a single occasion.

SCOTLAND: the best of a poor bunch

BY ALAN LORIMER

Gordon Simpson, who emerged as a key member of Scotland's back row, goes on the rampage against Australia.

If anything characterised the Scotland tour of Fiji and Australia last summer it was the introduction of southern hemisphere players into the Scottish game at the top level. Of the 35 players selected for the tour party, five originated from south of the equator and four of them went on to play in the two Tests against Australia.

Scotland had dipped their toes into this particular water back in 1989 when Sean Lineen was selected at centre for the national side to form what subsequently became a cap-record-breaking midfield partnership with Scott Hastings. That, however, was a blip – until, that is, this season. In going down the route of strengthening their squad with incomers, Scotland have now sent out a signal to disenchanted Scottish-qualified southern hemisphere players that the motherland will consider them seriously.

No newcomer played a more important onfield role than Scotland's tight-head Matthew Proudfoot, a former Northern Transvaal player with a rugby pedigree to match. Not since the era of the mighty Iain Milne have Scotland had a tight-head of Proudfoot's build and strength. Such was his impact on tour that many are predicting that the South African could be in for a long innings.

Proudfoot was one of two players to arrive in Scotland at the start of 1998. The other was Gordon Simpson, a former North Harbour and Wellington player, whose on-the-ball game appealed to the instincts of

Scotland tour coach Jim Telfer. So much so that the New Zealander displaced the impressive Adam Roxburgh and found himself one of the key players in a Scotland back row that gave as good as it got.

The other southern hemisphere debutant in the Scotland team for the first Test was Glenn Metcalfe, the 27-year-old Glasgow Hawks player, who hails from Waikato. Metcalfe took his chance against New South Wales, showing his attacking skills from the

Left: Scotland lock Scott Murray tries to evade Australia's Tim Horan. A mobile forward, Murray was a success Down Under and paired up well in the boiler room with the equally mobile Stuart Grimes.

Below: Scotland's Rowen Shepherd is caught during the tourists' clash with Victoria. Shepherd, who has switched from full back to centre, created his country's only try in the two Tests against the Wallabies.

full-back position. There are still a few raw edges to be smoothed out, but the signs are that Metcalfe may offer Scotland what Andy Irvine did a couple of decades ago.

Scotland's eight-match tour, however, was not a trade fair for southern hemisphere players. Essentially it was about developing players for the 1999 World Cup, in which respect Telfer and his fellow coaches can only be satisfied with the outcome. Notably so in the second row, where the improvement made by the relatively lightweight lock pairing of Stuart Grimes and Scott Murray was impressive. Both are highly mobile players and against Australia were key components in a defensive strategy that frustrated the Wallabies' offensive game.

Another player who emerged with plaudits from the tour was Rowen Shepherd, the erstwhile Scotland full back who is resurrecting his international career at inside centre after seemingly dropping out of favour. Shepherd's determined running created the only try the Scots achieved in two Tests against the Wallabies, who themselves ran in nine scores. And that was the telling statistic. Scotland defended well, competed up front, but never looked remotely like toppling the Australians, despite the presence of the Lions stand-off Gregor Townsend, happily restored to the No. 10 position by the Scotland coaches.

No one was more honest than Scotland's skipper Rob Wainwright, who for the umpteenth time in his career at the helm had to admit that his side finished second by more than a short head. Speaking after the second Test in Brisbane, Wainwright said, 'What it came down to was that we were playing against a side who were better than us. But I would never fault the team for effort.'

Even allowing for the fact that this was not a full-strength Scotland side (but in no way as unrepresentative as the crew that featured in England colours), the gap in standards is alarming. The most worrying aspect was Scotland's inability to pose any real threat in attack. In the first Test against the Wallabies the picture was blurred by the shoulder injury to hooker Gordon Bulloch that forced an underprepared Kevin McKenzie to come on as a sixth-minute substitute. On the day, the line out was a shambles, and while not accepting the total blame, McKenzie acknowledged that his throwing-in had not been of the required standard.

A week later McKenzie sorted out his problems, and Scotland's line out worked like clockwork. But the resultant flow of possession delivered to the backs served only to confirm the earlier-formed view that it is in back play that Scotland are lagging behind the likes of Australia and New Zealand. The difference was in the handling skills, the individual pace and the more imposing physical presence of the Wallaby back line. This comparison was also made in the wake of the embarrassing defeat by Fiji in the first game of the tour.

Scotland coach Jim Telfer believes that Fiji's victory was to do with a gap in skill levels between southern hemisphere sides and those (apart from France) from north of the equator. Telfer suggested that southern hemisphere sides possess far superior handling skills because they play and practise in good conditions for so much of their season. The conclusion he draws is that countries like Scotland should seriously consider playing rugby in the summer months – if not at adult level then certainly in the younger age groups. 'We have a similar climate in our summer to winter in Australia. That would be the time of year to develop the skills of youngsters instead of on a freezing November night. I would like to see far more summer rugby. Gavin Hastings, after all, has been talking about it for years, but it would be difficult to make the change,' said Telfer.

The 55-26 Fiji defeat, however, also had much to do with bad planning. With hindsight the whole Fiji exercise had 'disaster' hanging over it in large neon lights. It was meant to be a tough precursor to the Australian part of the tour. In the event it was tough all right, but tough off the pitch as well. Privately a number of the Scottish players were dismayed at the logistical arrangements for what was after all a full-blown Test match against Fiji and not some kind of missionary visit. These arrangements entailed professional players having to play a Test match after flying into an alien climate and then enduring a miserably long bus journey on the eve of the game – on the face of it quite unacceptable.

Fortunately the tourists were able to recover from the shock of defeat with three straight wins against Victoria in Melbourne, New South Wales Country XV in Bathurst, and, the real scalp, New South Wales in Sydney. The 34-10 victory over the Waratahs seemed to have put the tour back on course and confirmed the readiness of full back Glenn Metcalfe and flanker Gordon Simpson to play at full Test level. The effect of Scotland's win was as immediate as it was bizarre, New South Wales coach Matt Williams going straight to the Scots dressing room to dissociate himself from the hostile media comments that had been thrown at the Scotland tourists. 'I want to apologise for all the things the press have been saying,' he said. Scotland's captain Rob Wainwright stated, 'Some of the criticism through the week got to the boys. That was why we came out like a whirlwind today.'

Scotland's midweek side all but gave the Test team a pre-international lift with a stirring performance against the Australian Barbarians at Penrith, the second-string Scots fighting back strongly, only to lose 39-34. A week later the midweekers once again lost by a five-point margin, this time against Queensland at Ballymore. Once again a strong second-half performance brought them back into a match that seemed to have run away from them in the opening period of play.

If there were glaring deficiencies in Scotland's offensive game, then there was some compensation to be derived from the tourists' defensive effort in both Tests – particularly in the second Test at Ballymore, where Scotland's midfield tackling shut out the very potent threat of Daniel Herbert and Tim Horan. Scotland also showed a quickness to the breakdown points, an area of the tourists' game that had Wallaby coach Macqueen conducting a pre-Test campaign that accused the Scots of illegal tactics in preventing quick delivery of the ball.

Wallaby lock forward Tom Bowman runs into the Scotland half backs. Scotland showed good defensive qualities in both Tests but lacked penetration in attack.

It was a one-sided war of words, but one that finally forced Rob Wainwright to speak out, the Scotland captain suggesting that English referee Brian Campsall, who awarded a succession of penalties against the Scots in breakdown situations, had been taken in by the Macqueen propaganda. Speaking after the second Test, Wainwright said, 'I'm getting sick of the way Rod Macqueen's hype has got to the referee. Quite frankly his comments have riled me. But today Campsall fell for them. We are babes when it comes to killing the ball compared to some of the international teams we play against.'

Babes perhaps in other areas of the game as well. But Scotland's 'babes' will need to grow up rapidly if the national side is to compete in the next World Cup. The tour pointed to an upswing in fortunes. But only if promise becomes achievement will Scotland's journey to the other side of the globe be judged a complete success.

Elite sponsor of the England rugby team.

Call 0800 21 4000 for details of what we can do for you.

cellnet network

cellnet it's in your hands

TELECOM SECURICOR CELLULAR RADIO LIMITED.

PREVIEW OF THE SEASON 1998–99

THE FIVE NATIONS CHAMPIONSHIP

BY BILL McLAREN

The celebrations begin at the Stade de France after Raphael Ibanez's side become the first French team to win successive Grand Slam titles.

Those who have expressed concern that not only is there a gulf in class between the northern and southern hemispheres but also in the Five Nations Championship between France and England on the one hand and the Celtic nations on the other found supportive evidence in the 1998 Five Nations. It delivered a record 55 tries and again was dominated by France and England. France beat Scotland by 51-16 and Wales by 51-0; England churned out 34 points against Scotland, 35 against Ireland and 60 against Wales.

Raphael Ibanez's side created their own niche as the first from France to win a Grand Slam for the second season in a row, and they did so with a remarkable tries differential of 18 scored and three conceded. England achieved a fourth consecutive Triple Crown, a 21st Triple Crown in all, and 146 points in the four games of the championship – all new records. As if to underline their superiority, England are unbeaten by any of the other home unions for four seasons. Their last such reverse was at the hands of Ireland (12-13) at Twickenham on 19 February 1994.

It was hardly surprising, therefore, that the France v England meeting on the opening day of the 1998 championship, and the first international at the new venue of Stade de France in Paris, was generally regarded as a likely championship decider. It turned out to be just that, for, at the climax to the tournament, England would have been declared champions on points differential had Wales managed to beat France at Wembley. The Welsh never looked like doing so, and France collected a record 12th outright championship and brought their slams tally to six.

That French achievement was all the more remarkable in that, in November, prior to the championship, they had been put to the sword by the touring Springboks at Parc des Princes. The margin of 52-10 created astonishment in the rugby world. Could anyone have imagined that France ever would concede seven tries in a cap international? Typically the French came back with all guns blazing and with characteristic panache.

France, of course, fielded a distinguished management/coaching team – Jo Maso (manager), Jean-Claude Skrela and Pierre Villepreux (coaches). Those three had played together for France – Maso as one of the most gifted and adventurous midfield magicians; Skrela and Villepreux as clubmates in a Toulouse side that embraced a spectacular and daring style. So there was not much doubt how the French squad under their guidance would play nor that they would select the players with the right equipment for following that pattern. Thus some famous names were missing from the squad in which they placed their faith – no Thierry Lacroix, Olivier Merle or Laurent Cabannes. There was, however, the advantage of consistency of selection, for only one change was made – Xavier Garbajosa on the wing for Christophe Dominici – in the original selections for the four games. It was a side possessed of all round pace, too, not least at loose forward, where Olivier Magne and the Lievremont brothers, Marc and Thomas, were ideally equipped for fluent play. The Lievremonts, whose family of seven brothers and one sister all played rugby, became the first brothers since 1972 to play together for France.

Philippe Bernat-Salles scores against Scotland. He almost joined compatriots Patrick Estève and Philippe Sella in scoring in all four games, but missed out against Wales.

Yet it was scrummaging that was at the heart of France's 24-17 win over England. The French front row, with captain Ibanez bracketed by two solid citizens, Christian Califano and Franck Tournaire, caused acute discomfort to England's scrummage and so neutralised an England strength area of the loose forwards and scrum half Kyran Bracken. Not only that but the French line out won all their own ball and ensured that on four occasions England would make no profit from their own throw. Without a reliable set-piece platform, it said something for English resolve that not only did they drive over

Neil Back for their only try but were still very much in contention at 21-17 until Jean-Luc Sadourny popped over a dropped goal to clinch victory for France very much as Thomas Castaignède had done two years previously.

It was in the France v England match that the French wing Philippe Bernat-Salles, known as the 'Pau Rocket', took the first step towards a possible place in rugby lore with one of France's two tries. Having subsequently shot in for two against Scotland and one against Ireland, he required just one try against Wales to join that illustrious quartet – Carston Catcheside of England (1924), Johnny Wallace of Scotland (1925), Patrick Estève of France (1983) and Philippe Sella of France (1986) – as the only players to have scored a try in each of the four games of a Five Nations championship. Against Wales, however, Bernat-Salles came so near, yet so far, to finish try-less.

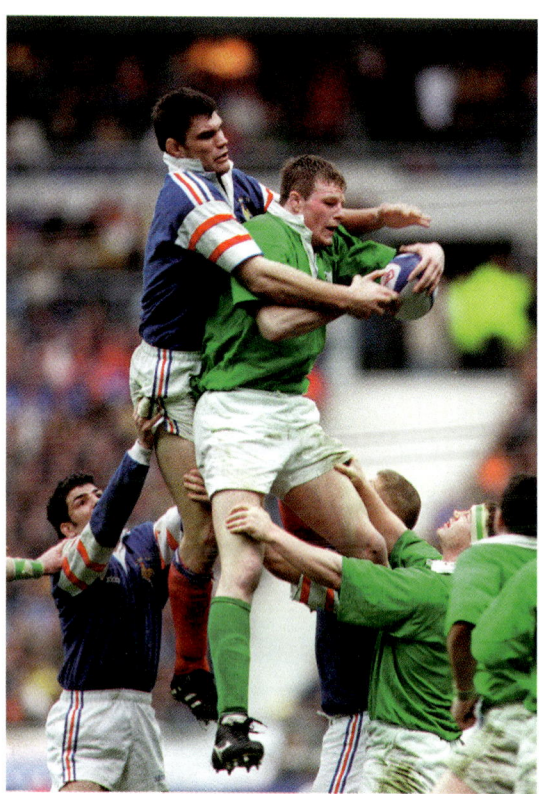

Malcolm O'Kelly gathers for Ireland despite the attentions of France's Fabien Pelous. O'Kelly was one of the successes of a season in which Ireland frightened France but ended up with the wooden spoon and a whitewash.

In their game against Scotland at Murrayfield, in which Tony Stanger led out the Scots to mark his 50th cap appearance, the French turned on the style, and none more so than Olivier Magne, who capped a wonderful performance with an inch-perfect grubber kick at pace that was as meat and drink to Bernat-Salles, who burned the grass in scoring the try. Having set up Bernat-Salles with a huge left-handed miss pass for his first try, it could be said that Magne had been a huge influence on French fortunes!

France scored six tries to one in their 51-16 victory over the Scots, which might have caused them subconsciously to underestimate the Irish a fortnight later in Paris. It had to be something of an irony that Ireland, with a new coach in the former New Zealand hooker Warren Gatland, should come close to recording what would have been the shock of the tournament against France, yet finished the campaign with their first 'whitewash' since 1992. In fact Ireland's form was hardly reflected in that wooden spoon, for they lost their first two matches to Scotland and France by only one and two points respectively. Against France they raised some hope that perhaps the gulf between the heavyweights and the Celts was not quite so wide after all. Certainly in Paris they demonstrated that heart, self-belief and passion could counter pace and skills. Every Irishman tackled like the crack of doom, their scrum half, Conor McGuinness of St Mary's College, excelled in cover and fringe probe and the Irish forwards showed that, on their day and even without their British Isles lock, Jeremy Davidson, they could, as the Scots would say, 'rummle up' any other eight. Malcolm O'Kelly proved an impressive stoke-room partner for Patrick Johns, and a comparative unknown, New Zealand-born flanker Andrew Ward from the Ballynahinch Club, signalled his new cap status with one early bone-jarring torpedoing of that class act Magne. France's winning margin was just 18-16.

The French then made their first acquaintance with Wembley Stadium, with a Grand Slam on offer if they could trim Wales. This they did with an awesome display of high-speed teamwork for their biggest championship victory and Wales' biggest championship defeat. The margin was 51-0, the result of the French working ball brilliantly out of the tackle, churning back a shoal of quick later-phase possession so that the ball carrier inevitably had choices, and producing a display of sheer genius from the baby-faced assassin Thomas Castaignède. When he and his wily half-back partner, Philippe Carbonneau, were substituted after 68 minutes they were accorded a standing ovation by friend and foe alike.

It was a heavy blow to Wales that they had to take on the French without their former Rugby League midfield duo, Allan Bateman and Scott Gibbs, but throughout the campaign the potential of the Welsh back division seldom was fully exploited and there was uncertainty over where to play Neil Jenkins. He was at full back against England and at stand-off for the other three games, where he did bring an element of orchestration, although his lack of sizzling acceleratory pace was cruelly exposed by Castaignède. Jenkins, however, had a field day in the 30-21 defeat of Ireland at Lansdowne Road with 20 points. His final all-in total is 594 in 57 cap internationals, which places him fourth in the list of the world's top international scorers behind Michael Lynagh (911), Gavin Hastings (667) and Grant Fox (645). The average points per game of those three respectively is 12.6, 10.9 and 14; Jenkins' is 10.4.

England, meanwhile, bounced back from defeat by France with eight tries in their 60-26 demolition of Wales at Twickenham. The former South African World Cup captain, François Pienaar, reckoned that that was the best he had ever seen England play. Their tight forwards, including the 19st 12lbs Phil Vickery of Gloucester, gave them a solid base in set piece and ruck/maul; their loose forwards, captain Lawrence Dallaglio, Richard Hill and Neil Back, revelled in achieving the right mix of drive and spin; and the Sale wing David Rees combined brilliantly with Jeremy Guscott and Will Greenwood, as well as scoring two tries.

This England also fought back from 6-12 down to two tries by Bateman and were out of sight at 32-12 by half-time. Paul Grayson not only collected 20 points but underlined a new attacking dimension to his performance that marked him out as one of the most improved players in the tournament. He was also a prolific source of points: 12 against France, 20 against Wales, 19 against Scotland that comprised all four scoring methods (try, dropped goal, penalty and four conversions) and 15 against Ireland for 66 points to give him an all-in total of 210 in 15 games. Neil Back also showed his class as one of the most effective hunting dogs of the tournament, besides scoring tries against France and Wales, and Michael Catt showed his versatility in playing at full back against France, replacement stand-off against Wales and wing against Ireland.

Thomas Lievremont crosses for France against Wales, watched by a helpless Neil Jenkins. Thomas was part of an outstanding French back row that also featured his brother Marc and Olivier Magne.

England recorded their fifth consecutive win over Scotland at Murrayfield by 34-20, despite having been held to 6-6 at half-time. They opted for scrummages instead of penalties on four occasions and gained a penalty try for scrummage collapse before leaking two late tries to Tony Stanger and New Zealand-born Shaun Longstaff. Stanger thus equalled the Scottish record of 24 cap international tries held since 1933 by the famous 'Flying Scot', Ian Smith. One unusual feature of the game was the deft chip ahead by Scotland's large lock forward Damian Cronin to force a close-range line out, which England's frontal expertise ensured did not result in a Scottish try.

England brought their tries differential in the championship to 17 scored and 10 conceded with a 4 tries to 2, 35-17 win over Ireland at Twickenham that consigned Ireland to an eighth post-war whitewash. This was another spirited and committed Irish forward display, their rucking highly effective. Keith Wood, O'Kelly and Ward were especially impressive, and Ireland actually held England to 10-10 in the second half. England did not seek width often enough and they were cut back to 25-17 by Denis Hickie's second try, but they had the edge at forward and there was evidence of a developing rapport between Guscott and Greenwood in centre.

With their wins over Scotland at Wembley and Ireland at Lansdowne Road, Wales might have challenged for the championship. However, France put paid to such aspirations with their seven tries to none annihilation at Wembley, Wales finishing with the worst tries differential of the championship: 8 scored, 19 conceded.

Having suffered grievously at the hands of Australia (8-37), South Africa (10-68) and Italy (21-25), Scotland hinted at revival with their 17-16 win in Dublin, where they have not lost since 1988. The Irish took the scrummage honours by persuading the renowned Scottish coach, Jim Telfer, to substitute Bath loose-head David Hilton for Newcastle's George Graham, who had found, as sundry others had discovered, not least some large fellows in South Africa, that the British Isles tight-head, Paul Wallace, is a singularly awkward customer against whom to lock horns.

The Scots, however, were outrun by the French, who did everything at impressive pace; scored two tries to one yet still lost to Wales; and were beaten by England for the ninth season in a row. Yet in full back Derek Lee of London Scottish, Cameron Murray of

Jeremy Guscott, winning his 50th Test cap, takes on Wayne Proctor in England's 60-26 victory over Wales. Although a menace in midfield, Guscott could not get on the scoresheet, try as he might.

Hawick, Longstaff, hooker Gordon Bulloch of West of Scotland, lock Stuart Grimes of Watsonians and Kelso flanker Adam Roxburgh, they blooded young players for future campaigns. Roxburgh had a notably fine match as open-side flanker against England.

Ireland's wooden spoon was an unfair reflection on their forwards, who responded to the fire and fury of their captain, Keith Wood, to make all their rivals pull out all the stops. However, Ireland had a shortage of class along their back division and also of pivotal direction, although wing Denis Hickie (St Mary's College) showed his eye for the main chance with a try against France and two against England.

France were worthy champions, capable of striking hard on any front. They were blessed with power and guile up front, rare pace in their back three and in their breakaway unit, and all revelled in what coach Villepreux refers to as 'freedom to run'. Nor is there any doubt that the northern hemisphere challenge to southern rivals has to be spearheaded by France and England, with the Celtic nations having to look to all of their laurels and more in order to catch up. At full strength, and not so sadly bereft of class players as England have been recently in their visits to Australia, New Zealand and South Africa – and, to a lesser extent, as Scotland have been on tour in Fiji and Australia – France and England remain the big guns of the Five Nations, as they demonstrated in the 1998 championship.

Scotland open-side flanker Adam Roxburgh steps on the gas as England's Garath Archer struggles to close him down. Roxburgh shone against England and was selected for Scotland's summer tour of Fiji and Australia.

a stirring experience

"Our aim is **excellence** both on and off the pitch.

Saracens' World Class Team work together to provide fast flowing, **entertaining** rugby. Our Stadium offers unrivalled facilities, whilst our staff make sure that **everyone** enjoys our unique match day experience.

Saracens - it's a great day out!"

home *of world class rugby* 98/99

SARACENS

Ticket Office 01923 496009
Club Shop 01923 496005
Office 01923 496200

Saracens Ltd, Vicarage Road Stadium, Vicarage Road, Watford, Herts. WD18ER

www.saracens-rfu.co.uk

KEY PLAYERS 1998–99

BY IAN ROBERTSON

ENGLAND

MATT PERRY

GARATH ARCHER

It is hard to believe that at the start of last season Matt Perry was not only uncapped but virtually unknown outside Bath. At the age of 20 he won his first England cap against Australia. Three weeks later he had won three more after two Tests against New Zealand and one against South Africa. This multi-talented young player seems to be equally comfortable at fly half, centre or full back. At Millfield he was a member of the England Schools squad and on leaving school he was soon chosen at fly half for England Colts. He rapidly made the transition to the England Under 21 side and toured Australia with them in the summer of 1997. He has played every position in the back division at Bath except scrum half and has had an outstanding first season in international rugby. He is at his best as an attacking full back, where he can exploit his speed and eye for a gap. He is strong and elusive and is equally adept at creating and scoring tries. He is solid in defence, good under the high ball and a sound tackler. After a season with England at full back he started the summer tour at centre against Australia. Wherever he plays he looks set for a long England career.

England have been able to select from real strength at lock forward during the 1990s. After Wade Dooley and Paul Ackford helped England collect the Grand Slam in 1991, Martin Johnson and Martin Bayfield did the same in 1995. Johnson is still there, and his new partner is Garath Archer. As the game has changed under the new laws so too has the role of the lock forward, and Archer seems to be exactly what the ideal modern lock should be. At 6ft 6ins, he is tall enough to win his share of line-out ball, and at 19 stones he makes a major contribution to the scrummage. Above all, he is mobile in the open, and in this important sphere of play he performs more like a No. 8 than a second row. He won his first England cap at 21 against Scotland in 1996 and went on to collect one more against Ireland in 1996 and a further eight in England's 1997-98 domestic season. Before making the full England team, he played for England Schools, England Colts, England Under 21 and Emerging England. He can thank his being part of a great Newcastle team for his early Test opportunities and looks certain to be in the England side for a long time to come.

FRANCE

THOMAS CASTAIGNEDE

RAPHAEL IBANEZ

In the past ten years the French have produced some wonderful threequarters, two great full backs and some brilliant back play, but they had not unearthed a really outstanding fly half in the past 25 years, until now. Thomas Castaignède enjoyed a fantastic season in the Five Nations Championship in 1998, and in the space of 12 months he has become the best fly half in the northern hemisphere. He won his first cap against Romania in 1995 as a centre and he went on that year to play Tests against Argentina and New Zealand. He has not yet played in a World Cup, but there is every possibility he will be one of the stars of the next tournament, which takes place in Europe in 1999. The English are only too well aware of his remarkable talents. He has played against them only twice, but he was a match winner on both occasions. In 1996 in Paris he dropped a goal late in the match to snatch victory, and he masterminded the French win over England at the new Stade de France in Paris in 1998 with a magnificent individual performance in which he made several lightning breaks. He has instant, blistering acceleration and a ready eye for a gap; he also kicks well and reads the game well – all of which makes him the best French fly half in living memory.

The French have boasted several good hookers in recent years. Raphael Ibanez probably would not be one of the very best, but his great strength is that he is an excellent captain. Over the years the French have often lost matches they should have won because of their lack of discipline and organisation. When the pressure is on and the match is delicately balanced they have displayed a knack of pressing the self-destruct button. All too often they have been the better team, but they have thrown the game away by conceding a lot of penalties and arguing not only with the referee but also among themselves. A strong captain can work wonders for the French. Jacques Fouroux led them to a Grand Slam in the late 1970s, and Jean-Pierre Rives was another inspirational captain in the 1980s. Ibanez could well prove to be in the same mould. He won his first cap as a replacement against Wales in 1996 and he won six more caps in 1997, most of them also as a replacement. However, in 1998 he replaced Marc Dal Maso as first-choice hooker and was also made captain. He led France to a handsome victory over England in Paris, and the French went on to complete their first ever back-to-back Grand Slams. His captaincy will be very important in World Cup year.

IRELAND

CONOR McGUINNESS

KEITH WOOD

The Irish have spent most of the past ten years looking to establish a pair of half backs and judging by the past couple of seasons, the search is still on. However, with the World Cup only 12 months away it would make a great deal of sense to choose Conor McGuinness at scrum half for this season and stick with him right through to the end of 1999. He has shown immense promise since he won his first cap against New Zealand in Dublin in November 1997 and he has a solid rugby pedigree. He played two years in the Irish Schools side and went on tour with them in 1992 to Australia. He played for St Mary's College and went to University College Dublin. Following the traditional Irish ladder to the top, he won caps for the Ireland Under 21 side and provincial selection for Connacht. He has partnered Eric Elwood regularly for Connacht and Ireland, and there is every chance that given an extended run they could be the answer to Ireland's long-running half-back problem. McGuinness is very quick on the break with a good eye for a gap, and despite his lack of bulk he is a strong runner. He has a good, quick, accurate pass and he is also a decent kicker. He links well with his back row and he could become the fulcrum of the Irish side.

The Irish forwards proved their worth not only in the domestic championship but also on the British Lions tour to South Africa in 1997. Three Irish forwards became first-choice selections for the Lions Test team: prop Paul Wallace, lock Jeremy Davidson and hooker Keith Wood. Wood is unquestionably one of the best hookers in the world and he can even be compared favourably with the legendary All Black Sean Fitzpatrick. Like Fitzpatrick he looks the part at 6ft and almost 17 stones and he is a tremendously mobile forward who excels with the ball in his hands. He can be quite devastating in open play. He runs around the field more like a flanker than a front-row forward. He is tough and competitive in the scrums, a very good thrower-in of the ball at the line out and a decisive tackler in defence. He won his first cap against Australia in 1994 and he made his mark in the World Cup in 1995. He has been captain of Ireland for the past two years and he is every bit the inspirational captain leading from the front. If Ireland do well in the build-up to the 1999 World Cup, it will be because they have a very good pack and a very good captain.

SCOTLAND

GARY ARMSTRONG

ROB WAINWRIGHT

The new professional era has meant that any really dedicated player can devote himself totally to rugby and benefit from the opportunity to train seven days a week to ensure peak fitness right through a long and demanding season. Gary Armstrong has flourished in this situation. It is amazing to think he won his first cap for Scotland more than ten years ago, against Australia in 1988. He is now 32 years old, but amazingly he is the youngster in the Newcastle half-back partnership. His fly half, Rob Andrew, is 35 years of age, and it is no accident that these two very experienced, wily campaigners were the inspiration behind Newcastle winning the Premiership last season. Gary Armstrong is playing some of the best rugby of his career and after having a complete rest during the summer he should be the guiding light as Scotland prepare for the World Cup in 12 months' time. He has always had a fast, accurate service and he has always kicked well from the base of the scrum and behind the line out. He is still lethal breaking from the scrum and even more so from rucks and mauls. He is devastating in attack and just as effective in defence, where his tackling is ruthless. He remains the perfect all round scrum half, and it will be in Scotland's best interest to build their back division around his many talents.

In some ways it is an indictment of the lack of talent coming through in Scotland that with the World Cup less than a year away the best two Scottish forwards remain Rob Wainwright and Doddie Weir. Their international careers both span more than half a dozen years, and they are by far the two most experienced players in the pack. Both have toured with the British Lions and both have played some great rugby at the highest level. It is essential for the Scots to try and build a pack around these two formidable players. Wainwright won his first cap against Ireland in 1992 and he has been an established member of the team ever since, although he has missed a lot of games through injury. He has played most of his best rugby in recent seasons at No. 8. However, he was quick enough in his Cambridge University days to play at open-side flanker and today he is equally effective at blind-side flanker. He has good hands, making him dangerous in attack, and he is a strong defensive player. He is also an exceptionally capable line-out jumper and this is a talent that Scotland will need to continue to exploit. He had one spell as captain for two years up until last season and he led Scotland again on their 1998 summer tour to Fiji and Australia. He certainly has 12 months of top-class rugby left in him.

WALES

ALLAN BATEMAN

COLIN CHARVIS

The Welsh had every reason to complain during the past 20 years as many of their best players switched to Rugby League. However, it was no surprise when Rugby Union went professional that many of these players switched back from League to strengthen Wales quite considerably. While the forwards who have returned have been very welcome, it is the two centres, Allan Bateman and Scott Gibbs, who have captured most of the headlines. No sooner were they back in Wales playing Rugby Union in the national side than they were selected for the British Lions tour of South Africa in 1997. Both made an enormous impact. Allan Bateman showed he is still quick and elusive at the highest level despite being 33 years of age and he is also a tremendous defensive player. He returned to international rugby for Wales in 1996 against South Africa, six years after he won his previous Welsh cap, against Namibia in 1990. He played the whole season for Wales in 1997 before going with the Lions to South Africa and looks sure to be a key player for Wales right through to the World Cup in 1999. The Welsh midfield looks solid and watertight in defence and full of exciting potential in attack. He has now won 16 Welsh caps and scored three tries. In the next 12 months he looks sure to increase both these totals.

That Wales failed to contribute a single first-choice forward for the British Lions Test team in South Africa in 1997 speaks volumes for the current lack of strength in the Principality. This was underlined in the Five Nations Championship in 1998 when the Welsh pack was swept aside by both England and France, leading in both cases to resounding defeats for Wales. If the Welsh are to be a force in the 1999 World Cup, they will have to build a new pack to give their back division a chance. There is no doubt they have a very good set of backs, but they hardly featured in attack in the Five Nations because they had to operate on limited rations. The main hope for Wales is to build a pack around a useful back row, which is spearheaded by Colin Charvis. He won his first cap when he came on as a replacement against Australia in 1996 and he won his next cap when he played the whole game against South Africa the following month. He has been an established member of the team ever since, although he missed the England international in 1997 and the British Lions tour because of a knee injury. He is a big, fast, strong forward with good hands and he is also a good defensive player. Although he has played blind-side flanker and No. 8 for Wales, his recent selection at open-side surely places him in his best position.

**THE WORLD'S FAVOURITE
TOMATO KETCHUP**

THE CLUB SCENE

ENGLAND – Too many foreigners?

BY BILL MITCHELL

A year ago it was obvious that the domestic game in England had become a mass of contradictions, and in the intervening dozen months nothing has changed. The standard in the top leagues has never been higher, the internal quarrels in the Twickenham offices remain unresolved and the headlong rush of too many clubs towards bankruptcy continues. All these are, of course, separate issues, but all are connected, and the combined story leaves the English 'bottom line' looking in reality in very poor shape. It is all very well to be able to report that some marvellous rugby is regularly on offer, but again one must ask, 'At what cost to the English game?'

If the national team's competitive season had ended with the victory over Ireland at Twickenham in April, it would have been possible to say that things were not too bad. However, since then the England team has been to the southern hemisphere with such disastrous consequences that it will need a miracle for a quick recovery to be effected.

Who and what were to blame? The answer has to be that anyone involved in planning the international future of English rugby and the wellbeing of the game at the top must accept a share of the responsibility. The club owners are clearly more interested in gaining satisfactory returns on their own investments and the prestige that goes with their clubs' successes. To them any international commitments that jeopardise that situation must be resisted. They employ the players, so they assume the right to decide where and when they play and for whom.

One can see their selfish point, but where does that leave England? And can the national team enjoy any prolonged success if their own union can no longer enforce its own decisions? How can a weakened touring party gain any benefit from a series of horrific drubbings? If clubs are allowed to fill their teams with imported talent how can native English players progress? Before the touring party even left this country, the claim that there was strength in depth had already been exposed through heavy defeats suffered by the 'A' team against the All Blacks, France, Wales and Scotland. With many top players unable to travel, there was no adequate cover. The Under 21 side had enjoyed some success, but most of the players were promising novices and still learning the trade.

The flooding of the top sides with brilliant and conscientious foreigners can only work out if the club officials see the imports as a temporary measure (and nothing more than that) while their novices gain experience, but there is little to suggest that those same officials intend to abandon the policy as soon as they have found English replacements. Only bankruptcy will halt the trend and that in itself will bring further disasters.

French international back Thierry Lacroix in action for Harlequins. Wonderful to watch, but are there too many foreign imports in the leagues for the good of the English game?

One suspects that the two Cassandras of the English game – Cliff Brittle and Fran Cotton – are among the few who realise the inherent dangers to the national wellbeing, the club ethos and the importance of even the apparently least important small-time club member, and they are being roundly abused by too many enthusiasts who think that the game in England has a licence to print money. References regularly made about King Canute merely demonstrate historical ignorance and a reckless desire to spend funds that just will not exist once the money men fold their tents and creep away. People are living in fools' paradises. The day of reckoning must come sooner rather than later and where do we go from there?

It is a bleak scene, but despite the doom and gloom in financial and administrative matters, most games I attended provided great entertainment. The competitive nature of the season and interest in it were both maintained until the final day, with top honours going to Newcastle, promoted only in 1997, after a brilliant win at Harlequins in the season's last Allied Dunbar match. Victory meant that they overtook Saracens, who had been their sole challengers for the title from early in the New Year.

Saracens had the consolation of winning the Tetley's Bitter Cup at Twickenham on the season's penultimate Saturday by a massive score (48-18) against Wasps, who have yet to win the competition after three losing finals and never looked like retaining their league title. In fact, at times they were relegation candidates.

Both Newcastle and Saracens had veteran stars who were enjoying 'Indian winters'. Newcastle were inspired by a slowing but canny genius in Rob Andrew, ably assisted by the likes of Pat Lam, Alan Tait, Doddie Weir, Gary Armstrong and a string of brilliant supporting stars. Saracens won the cup with superb farewell performances from Michael Lynagh and Philippe Sella, aided by François Pienaar, Danny Grewcock and skipper Tony Diprose – to name but a few. When the two teams met at Watford in league action, almost 20,000 were there, which proved that only success pays off.

A long distance away in terms of points were Bath and Leicester, with Northampton, Sale and Gloucester enjoying satisfactory campaigns. Harlequins continued to underperform and next season must hope that Zinzan Brooke will bring some All Black

Newcastle and Ireland prop Nick Popplewell salutes his try – Newcastle's third – in the championship-clinching victory over Harlequins in the season's final Allied Dunbar match.

magic to bear to effect a recovery.

Another sign of the professional times was the summary way in which Leicester dispensed with the services of Bob Dwyer, their successful Australian coach. Dean Richards will hope that he can bring home some kind of bacon or else his long association with the Tigers will end in tears. There is no room for sentiment these days.

Bath did win something big – the European crown, after a dramatic win in Toulouse against holders Brive. However, there were two sour notes associated with Bath's triumph. First, the top English clubs decided for their own reasons that Europe was not for them. An increase in the size of the Premiership top division was their solution to financial problems and only time – and the fans – will tell if this is wise. No one is indispensible – not even an English club.

The other nasty feature of Bath's season was an unsavoury incident at the Recreation Ground when London Scottish were the visitors in a Tetley's Bitter Cup match. The Australian flanker Simon Fenn had serious damage done to an ear by an alleged bite, and initially it seemed that Bath wanted to sweep the matter under the nearest carpet. Inevitably, there was an inquiry by the RFU, which placed the blame on the Bath prop Kevin Yates, who was duly suspended for six months despite protestations of innocence. Bath, who survived that cup game narrowly but went out at home to Leicester in the next round, eventually reinforced the penalty with one of their own. However, they won themselves few friends with their apparent unwillingness to act and they might well have done themselves no harm if they had poured scorn on various ludicrous public explanations that merely served to muddy the waters.

With the increase in size of the Premiership's top division – were not the players supposed to be playing too much rugby already according to their bosses? – there was no automatic relegation. London Irish and Bristol, the bottom clubs, had to play off against Rotherham and London Scottish respectively to retain their status. London Irish survived comfortably on aggregate, but Bristol, who had suffered a disastrous season, made way for London Scottish, who will share the Harlequins ground in the new season. The Exiles co-tenants at the Richmond Athletic Ground have decided that the best place for a club of their name to be based is Reading! One wonders how many loyal members will follow them in their bold move. Bedford had an outstanding season in the Premiership second division and were promoted along with West Hartlepool, who narrowly squeezed out London Scottish for the other automatic place.

Elsewhere there were three Jewson National Leagues, which produced plenty of excitement and worthy champions in ambitious Worcester (Division One), Birmingham Solihull (Two North), and another ambitious outfit, Camberley (Two South). Any league system that can reward initiative and ambition must be good for the game as long as the clubs do not go overboard on expenditure to achieve their aims.

Bedford scrum half Aadel Kardooni gets his kick away in the face of London Scottish pressure. Bedford, who also starred Rory Underwood, were champions of the Premiership second division after an outstanding season. The Exiles also went up to division one, defeating Bristol in the play-offs.

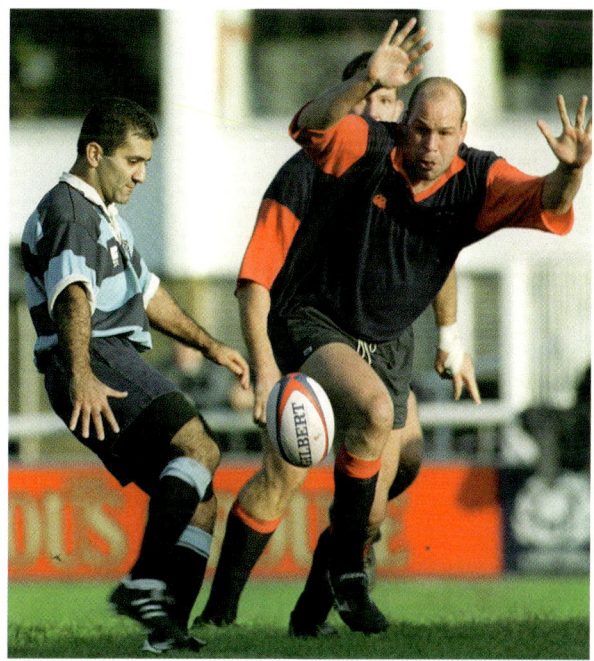

With relegation cancelled, interest in the divisional leagues concentrated solely on who would become senior clubs in the new season. The competition for promotion was intense, with New Brighton winning the closest battle of all by beating Doncaster to the North One title on points difference after match figures had been the same at 36 points each.

Whitchurch won the Midlands' top league with slightly more to spare and become Shropshire's first senior club, while Norwich gained the same distinction in their own county by taking the London and South East top honours narrowly from ambitious Staines. Finally, the South West Division's new seniors are not a West Country club but Bracknell from Berkshire, who outstripped Launceston from Cornwall by three points.

Cambridge were victors in the University Match at Twickenham for a fourth successive year, winning by a comfortable 29-17 margin. Oxford could not cope with the Light Blue rolling mauls inspired by the veteran lock Richard Bramley, playing in his fifth and (Oxford hope) last Blues encounter. Oxford's Nick Booth scored the best try of the match when the result was virtually settled and Oxford might have done better if Australian flanker David Kelaher had been able to land some simple penalty chances before half-time.

There were two questionable features of this match. First, Cambridge brought on two late replacements, presumably so that they could win well-deserved Blues. Why not award Blues in future to everyone in the final squad and avoid this unnecessary situation?

The second was some thoroughly unwelcome interference from the RFU. An honourable and honest tradition has it that the University Match touch judges should be the previous year's captains (or other officials if the former captains are not free to attend). The RFU insisted this tradition should be abandoned. Is nothing sacred? And in any case why should the RFU impose its own conditions on what is a private match and one of the few remaining genuinely amateur occasions – an occasion which, incidentally, brings in some welcome extra funds to Twickenham? The erosion of traditions is not a pleasant sign of the times.

The BUSA title was won comfortably by Swansea against Northumbria University at Twickenham, with HQ on the same day also seeing the women's university honours go outside England to Edinburgh University. A new outfit called Imperial Medicals won the Hospitals Cup from Guy's & St Thomas's, but for this competition to survive in a plausible manner there must be some new blood to take the place of the traditional teams, which have disappeared from the tournament. The Army retained the Inter-Services title, with – on paper – comfortable wins over the Navy at Twickenham and the RAF at Gloucester, but it is sad to see that three enjoyable services occasions at HQ have been reduced to one.

The Barbarians are being gradually squeezed out by the needs of the professional game and they were restricted to only three outings. It would be tragic if yet another honourable organisation were to disappear because no room can be found in the modern era of fixture congestion and indifference to the basic ethos of rugby.

On the credit side, Twickenham staged excellent matches to conclude the County Championship season, with Cheshire pipping Cornwall 21-14 for the senior honours and East Midlands beating Cumbria for the Under 21 title. Without Cornwall there might be no point in continuing this event, but the refreshing local 'nationalism' ensures decent crowds at the finals.

Headquarters also presented the Tetley's Bitter Vase final and the NPI Cup final for intermediate and junior teams respectively, and both were worthy of a better attendance on the day. Huddersfield YMCA beat West Leeds comfortably by 40-8 in the former match and must be commended on a thoroughly professional performance in the process, but Bedford Athletic's victory in the second game was desperately close, and Stroud might well have won had they not made a tactical error when victory seemed to be within their grasp. As it was, the match went to extra time, and the Midlanders won courtesy of Alf Bartlett's second try. The final score was 29-24, which gave Bedford Athletic a cup and league double, since they had also won the Midlands Second Division. Sadly, so far attendances at these intermediate and junior finals have been poor, so any fans in future who find themselves at a loose end are strongly recommended to try out this superb day – and the Daily Mail Schools Day in March for good measure.

The season did not quite end with the Middlesex 7s – there was still some vital league action left – but they did give the Barbarians the chance to show the public that they are still around. They beat Leicester in the final, but one must emphasise that the Barbarians do not exist merely to win 7s tournaments or represent Britain in such competitions internationally.

While holidays were being taken, the RFU AGM took place and Cliff Brittle was ousted in favour of Brian Baister as chairman. We must offer the newcomer our best wishes and hope that the top clubs will finally act in a responsible manner and realise that the welfare of the English international team as well as the small clubs at the grass roots of the game are both matters of importance. They may not believe it, but their own survival, where bankrupcy has not already arrived, depends on both entities flourishing.

A summary of the England scene must conclude that somehow the game manages to survive and with greatly improved standards at the top level, but at what price? Will the public continue to support clubs for ever if they rely on expensively imported players and make only token efforts to nurture home-grown talent? How long will the money men continue to support these extravagances? Are there contingency plans in any clubs' files to meet the moment when they cease to be subsidised and must fend for themselves? Who knows?

Catch me if you can! They (Stroud) couldn't, and Alf Bartlett touched down to help Bedford Athletic to victory in the NPI Cup final at headquarters.

SCOTLAND – Watsonians at last!

BY BILL McLAREN

Too often the bridesmaid, at last the bride! That sums up the fortunes of Edinburgh club Watsonians, who, having been runners-up in division one of Scotland's Premiership in the previous two seasons and also having lost in the cup final of 1996 to Hawick, at last broke through as undisputed division one champions of Scotland in 1997-98. They thus deprived the reigning champions, Melrose, of a third consecutive title by creating a closing situation in which Melrose had to beat Watsonians by 69 clear points to pip them at the post. Melrose did win that final contest, by 37-17, but few folk begrudged Watsonians their success, for under the coaching guidance of Andrew Ker (Scotland's stand-off against Wales and England in 1988), Peter Gallagher and (this season) David Cockburn, Watsonians had proved for some seasons the most exciting side in the championship, embracing a thoroughly attractive, attacking style from all parts of the pitch and with ball in hand. As the Glasgow Hawks dominated division two of the Premiership, and also won the cup final against Kelso by 36-14, it can be said that the cities had flexed their muscles and put their Border rivals, for a change, in their place!

A Kelso attack founders on the rock of Glasgow's defence in the SRU Tennants Velvet Cup final

The Premiership comprised divisions of ten teams, in which each played the others once on a home or away basis, the top five then forming Division A and playing each other once again on a home or away basis to decide positions one to five. The bottom five similarly formed Division B to decide positions six to ten. Four points were awarded for a win, two for a draw and there was a bonus point for a club scoring four or more tries in a match and for a club that lost by seven or fewer points.

Watsonians barely looked likely to don the mantle of champions when they lost two of their first five games to Jed-Forest (15-31) and Boroughmuir (12-14), the latter coached by the 29-times-capped Scottish centre Sean Lineen. They suffered another reverse at Burnbrae in January, their first national league or Premiership defeat by West of Scotland there since 1976. When they got all the cogs to mesh, however, Watsonians stitched together some gorgeous passages, notably in scoring 16 tries and conceding one in two games against Currie, who themselves had recorded a home victory by 20-17 against Melrose.

Two big results for Watsonians were their 33-24 success over Melrose on 14 February and their

34-8 defeat of West of Scotland on 26 April. In a riveting contest against Melrose that spawned four tries each, Watsonians capitalised on the absence through injury of Craig Chalmers and on an injury during the match to his successor, 15-times-capped Graham Shiel. They created a highly profitable rapport between their halves, Duncan Hodge and Graeme Burns, and their voracious loose-forward trio, Cameron Mather, Martin Waite and Nick Penny, of whom Hodge, Burns and Mather subsequently toured with Scotland in Fiji and Australia. So too did the 19-year-old centre Jamie Mayer, a powerfully built, blasting type, who thundered in for two tries against Melrose, and Stuart Grimes, a developing lock with pace and good hands, who gained his first cap against Ireland in Dublin on 7 February as replacement for Damian Cronin.

The match against West of Scotland at Myreside could have clinched the title for Watsonians, but they just failed to earn the crucial bonus point for four tries in their 34-8 victory, in which stand-off Duncan Hodge, capped against France, Australia and South Africa, scored all 34 points from three tries, five penalty goals and two conversions. The Watsonians pack were in rare form, the youngster Jason White, Scotland's Under 21 captain, joining with Grimes and Mather in creating line-out superiority, and Stuart Paul, the former Heriot's FP prop, giving an immense display at tight-head and in line-out support.

With such provision by their frontal troops, the Watsonians backs put together some glorious handling transference. Scott Hastings (Scotland's most-capped player with 65) operated at full back, Andrew Garry and the 19-year-old Marcus di Rollo formed, with Mayer, a rich blend in midfield, and Fergus Henderson and John Kerr were good footballers with a bit of zip on the wings. However, Watsonians' mobile forwards played an influential role in attack as underlined by the club's Premiership tries count – 29 of their 53 by their backs, 24 by the forwards. Yet when their rugged captain, hooker Grant McKelvey (capped against Australia), held the Premiership trophy aloft after that 37-17 defeat at Melrose on 2 May, it marked the end of an era, for 11 of that Watsonians side will play in the new super-districts set-up in 1998-99, a sad blow to the club game, since other sides will lose their star men in the same way.

Although Melrose, captained by their international No. 8, Carl Hogg, took some satisfaction from that 37-17 defeat of Watsonians, theirs was a disappointing season in which they suffered four Premiership defeats and were without their anchor man, Craig Chalmers, and their New Zealand flanker, Nick Broughton, for much of the campaign. Perhaps their full potential was realised only in their 49-7 margin over West of Scotland at Greenyards on 17 January after two Premiership defeats in a row from Hawick (8-19) and Currie (17-20). Against West, Scott Nichol, capped against Argentina in 1994 and generally a centre, was in marvellous form at full back, hitting the line at pace on several occasions and creating havoc in the West defence for a six tries to one advantage.

At full strength, Melrose, coached by the 44-times-capped Keith Robertson, had all the elements of a champion side with a powerful, driving pack in which the veteran Robbie Brown set a hard-working, inspirational example. The Melrose scrummage was strengthened late on by the arrival of the 20-stones Matthew Proudfoot from the Northern Transvaal Blue Bulls of South Africa. He made such an impact that he was chosen for Scotland's tour of Fiji and Australia in May and June. Melrose also had screeching pace on the wings from Chris Dalgleish and Mark Moncrieff, who shared 12 Premiership tries.

Four Premiership defeats, however, and the loss of the Scottish Cup they won last season were disappointing, although Melrose did have some consolation in winning their own prestigious 7s tournament in April with a 38-19 defeat of Watsonians in the final. So Watsonians became Scottish champions for the first time since winning the old unofficial championship in 1969-70, when they were coached by Mike Barrie, who just happened to be their 1997-98 club president!

The other big success story was written by the Glasgow Hawks, a 1997 amalgam of Glasgow Academicals, Glasgow High School FP and Kelvinside Academicals (GHK since 1982-83), who had an inspirational figure in that development in the former Glasgow Academicals and Scotland stand-off Brian Simmers. With Iain Russell, a former Kelvinside Academicals and Glasgow flanker, as coach, they assembled a powerful squad with a strong southern hemisphere element. Speedy, elusive wing-converted-to-full-back Glenn Metcalfe (whose grandmother came from Shawlands) is from Waikato but was born in Auckland, while gifted stand-off and goal-kicker Tommy Hayes and 18-stones tight-head prop Michael Beckham had both played World Cup qualifying Tests for the Cook Islands, although both were born in New Zealand.

Hayes directed operations with deft touch as well as scoring 184 points in 13 games (he also rattled on 170 points in 13 games for Glasgow's district side). There was experience and pace from the Scotland wing Derek Stark (who contributed 16 Premiership tries) and Chris Simmers in the centre; rugged defence from the captain, David Wilson, formerly of Currie; clever running angles from the other wing with the black scrumcap, Alastair Common; and high skill levels from Cameron Little and Stuart Simmers as the squad scrum halves. They operated behind a very strong pack, all of whom had played for Glasgow at district level and of whom Gordon McIlwham, the loose-head prop, was on the Scottish tour to Fiji and Australia. Gordon Mackay, in rumbustious form at No. 8, formed a formidable loose-forward trio with the Wallace brothers, Fergus and Murray, the latter having been capped against Australia, Wales and Italy in 1996-97.

Not only did the Hawks win the division two championship and promotion with just one defeat (5-14 against Kilmarnock, and that once the championship was decided and the Hawks were badly understrength) but they scored 521 points, close on 200 more than the next highest by Dundee High School FP.

Premiership excitement went to the wire as Heriot's FP sought to maintain their record of never having been out of division one since national leagues began in 1973-74. They cleared one hurdle by defeating Edinburgh Academicals 42-13, but then, as second bottom in Division 1B, they had to play off against Kelso (second top in 2A) at a neutral ground (Preston Lodge) for a place next season in the top division. Heriot's ran out victors by 33-12, by three tries to none, scored by Gregor Lawson, Vincent Payot and Jez Smith, so the Heriot's record still stands.

One of the season's curiosities was that the Scottish Rugby Union Velvet Cup final at Murrayfield on 9 May was contested by the champions and runners-up in division two. Glasgow Hawks had amassed 256 points at an average of 51 per game in seeing off Cumbernauld (92-6), Aberdeen Grammar School FP (39-10), then three division one sides, Jed-Forest (67-21), Watsonians (21-6) and Boroughmuir (37-12). Kelso scored 27 tries and conceded only six in beating Kinross (112-5), Murrayfield Wanderers (32-16), then three division one sides, West of Scotland (10-3), Melrose (18-13) and Currie (18-17). That defeat of Melrose was the shock result of the tournament, but Kelso, with Iain Fairley at centre and Adam Roxburgh at flanker giving a splendid lead, gave their vaunted rivals little room and scored two tries to one amid scenes of jubilation among their loyal support.

On finals day there was all the fun of the fair with a sky-dive simulator, a fun zone for youngsters, puppet shows, a creche, live music and a meet-the-players tent. Just under 25,000 attended.

In the cup final the rival stand-offs were from the southern hemisphere – Tommy Hayes and the South African Johnny Wearne. It was Wearne who put Fairley in for the opening try, which Wearne himself converted. Hayes, however, still just 23, began to demonstrate that ability to help colleagues to play, materialising wide out to send Stark racing over for the Hawks' first try. There were two others from Common and one typical scrummage pick-up score by Mackay. Hayes slotted four penalty goals and two conversions. Kelso's other points were from a try by Wearne, which he converted himself.

So the Glasgow Hawks, whose powerful pack laid the foundations, put Glasgow rugby firmly back on the map with that 36-14 cup-final win. At the same time their recruitment policy pointed the way for other Scottish clubs with financial clout to strengthen their squads with quality players, including some from the southern hemisphere. However, the Hawks themselves will have to recruit wisely as they lose their star men to the super-district arrangement that aims at providing Scotland's top performers with higher-quality rugby on a regular basis, thus to improve the nation's prospects at international level.

One other notable feat was performed by Selkirk in reaching the shield final for the third season running and in repeating their success of 1997 when they beat Biggar by 23-15. In 1996 they lost to Edinburgh Academicals by 28-21.

Joyous Glasgow Hawks supporters urge on their team against Kelso.

Cup winners Glasgow Hawks savour their moment of triumph after their 36-14 victory over Kelso. Kelso remained the Kings of Sevens, though, taking the Radio Borders/ Borders Toyota title for the third season running.

IT'S TIME YOU MADE THE CONVERSION.

When it comes to a winning team you can't beat Land Rover.

With the unmatched strength and endurance of Defender, the comfort and versatility of Discovery, the style and exuberance of Freelander and the sheer luxury of Range Rover, there's a Land Rover to suit every taste and requirement.

In addition, there's the excellent Freedom Finance package and, where status permits, Diplomatic concessions which means the best 4x4 by far is in a class of its own.

For more information call one of the numbers below and ask for Land Rover to see how they stand up to the test.

THE BEST 4x4xFAR

For details of your nearest Land Rover dealer call Freephone 0800 110 110
or write to - Land Rover, Freepost TK 494, Twickenham TW2 5UN.
Diplomatic Sales Hotline: 0181 410 8427

WALES – 1998: A watershed year

BY DAVID STEWART

South Africa 96, Wales 13. The Editor's brief is 'The state of rugby at club level'. Well, that scoreline tells all you need to know. The state of the nation is dire. And all this 12 months before rugby's biggest event comes to town. Humiliation is staring the hosts of Rugby World Cup in the face.

Make no mistake, players and punters at all levels hold the committee men of Westgate Street responsible. But do the committee men hear? Do they understand? And if so, what, if anything, do they intend to do about it? This article does not need to become an extended rant against the union. Simply put, in what other sphere of commercial or public life do the individuals at the top of the organisation survive a year-on-year downward spiral of achievement?

The year 1998 is a watershed. The fledgling professional game is in a mess at club and national level. RWC chairman Leo Williams is faxing Cardiff asking 'Will the stadium be ready in time?' The WRU seek a court injunction to stop local media from telling us such news. They are at legal war with Cardiff RFC. Some of the union's most famous clubs have gone perilously close to, or even beyond, the insolvency wall. Crowds are down, so are TV figures and there is a general lack of buzz about the game among the local population. A stop-go fixture list meant watching rugby was no longer habit-forming. For example, Cardiff v Bridgend has historically been a competitive, well attended local derby. This year's game at the Arms Park, before a depressingly thin crowd, was effectively men against boys after 20 minutes – a 60-point romp for the home side.

The only games that sparked genuine interest involved Swansea, Cardiff, Pontypridd and occasionally Ebbw Vale – coincidentally the finishing order of the top four in the (unsponsored) premier division. The All Whites were the deserving victors. John Plumtree, a Kiwi with experience in Natal, proved a shrewd choice as successor to Mike Ruddock. Led by Garin Jenkins and Stuart Davies effectively at forward, and playing with style behind in the persons of Arwel Thomas, Scott Gibbs and David Weatherley, Swansea were by some margin the most watchable and most complete side in the Principality. One particular source of pride was the provision of an entire back row of Davies, Appleyard and Charvis to the national team at one stage. These three were supported by the returning Paul Moriarty from Rugby League.

The key win was away to Cardiff in December – a game tinged with tragedy, as Gwyn Jones, the admired Welsh captain and open-side, suffered a neck fracture.

Swansea's Wales and British Lions centre Scott Gibbs was a key figure in the All Whites' successful league campaign.

A full recovery is still not certain, a chilling reminder of the dangers of this now high-impact contact sport. The return match at St Helens saw Swansea equally dominant up front, and that double largely accounted for the six-point margin (46 points to 40) that left Cardiff as runners-up.

Injuries hindered Swansea's progress in the Heineken Cup, although not before an understrength side went to Loftus Road on a sunny early season Sunday and ran Wasps desperately close for a quarter-final place. Cardiff had a better run in the European competition but somehow never seemed to fire on all cylinders. This ultimately led to the 'amicable' departure of Alex Evans back to Australia at the end of the season. The search for fresh blood as Director of Rugby ended with the promotion of Terry Holmes. Supporters fear little will change. The Blue and Blacks could field an all-international XV for most games, but fans often asked 'Where is the real quality?' The harsh answer was that beyond Rob Howley, Jon Humphreys, Leigh Davies and Canadian lock John Tait there was not much.

Cardiff travelled to Bath for their Heineken quarter-final, a 'return' match after last year's clash. The eventual competition winners turned the tables from 12 months earlier, but an assault by a visiting fan upon the referee at the final whistle left an unpleasant aftertaste. Cardiff's season never really seemed to recover, the club being bundled out of the SWALEC Cup away at Ebbw Vale. Their ongoing desire (with Swansea) to join the Allied Dunbar Premiership meant season-ticket holders received a letter saying in effect 'Please renew, even though we cannot tell you what the fixture list will be yet'. How many season tickets would Man Utd or Liverpool sell with a marketing pitch like that?

Pontypridd had another strong season. Their four battles with Brive – three on the field, one in a French bar – were compelling. The spirit and daring of their rugby won new admirers; their off-the-field activities probably didn't. Neil Jenkins is staying, despite a long-standing courtship with Bath. He and Paul John were, and continue to be, central to the club's success. Dennis John's coaching skills were recognised with his appointment as national caretaker for the doomed South African trip, prior to the appointment of Auckland's Graham Henry. Alas, no trophies for Ponty last season. Lack of capital makes it unlikely they will remain a force at the top level for very much longer.

Ebbw Vale were the season's breath of fresh air. Captained by a real personality in Kingsley Jones, they came fourth in the league and pushed Llanelli all the way in the cup final. Gwent rugby has long been a supporting pillar of the Welsh game. The decline of clubs like Pontypool and now the new-relegated Newport weakens the whole show and makes it vital that Vale continue to prosper. Former Neath No. 8 Mark Jones returned from League to bolster the forward effort, but regretfully continued to

Llanelli's Welsh international flyer Wayne Proctor tries to show Ebbw Vale a clean pair of heels in the SWALEC Cup final.

The Scarlets celebrate their 19-12 victory, in the SWALEC Cup final, one high point in a season in which money troubles saw them sell Stradey Park to the WRU.

demonstrate the unsavoury side of his game. A more welcome development was that of fly half Byron Hayward, who was capped in South Africa.

The Scarlets were the deserving cup winners. The final was held for the first and (one hopes, only) time out of Wales, at Bristol City FC. Llanelli's cup success was scant compensation for an otherwise disappointing time. Sixth position in the league and ongoing financial troubles resulted in the sale of their famous Stradey Park ground to the union. The WRU also had to take over the affairs of Neath. Their oldest club drifted into July receivership. Within weeks, Bridgend were declaring a £1 million debt. Relegated Newport did not spend big money. Chief Executive David Watkins, one of the few in charge who has experience of another professional game, was justifiably disgruntled that their good housekeeping resulted in a demise, while the less thrifty survived courtesy of the WRU financial lifeboat.

Question: Why so little coverage of the actual rugby from last year? Answer: Because so little of it seemed to matter. Week after week the back-page headlines reflected off-the-pitch activities. The future? Only a supreme optimist would predict a vibrant, well-attended professional (or even semi-pro) all-Welsh League. The cold reality of the modern era is that the WRU have ceded control in real terms, if not in constitutional ones just yet. Welsh clubs enter the 1998-99 season with more uncertainty and greater trepidation than in their previous 100 years or more. How many will survive the next 12 months as professional clubs? What, if any, European competition will they participate in? Can a depressing outlook be turned around, or will a prediction made at the time of professionalism in 1995 come true – namely that club rugby will go the way of soccer, with three or four Welsh-based teams in a predominantly English league? Will the stadium be ready? Will Graham Henry's appointment end in tears? Have the union only themselves to blame, or is it the inevitable march of progress in a harsh commercial world for which the local game was unprepared, and continues to be ill-equipped?

IRELAND – Shannon take four in a row

BY SEAN DIFFLEY

A fourth successive AIB league title for Shannon, who beat Garryowen in the knockout final after topping the table by five points.

Once again it was Shannon, the Irish club of the year – for the fourth consecutive season. And not only did they win the AIB All-Ireland League for 1997-98, they did it twice! Last season the administrators decided that the teams that finished the league campaign in the first four places should compete in a knockout finale, with the top league finisher playing the fourth-placed, and the second- and third-placed sides contesting the other semi-final.

Shannon, understandably, were less than enchanted with the format. They finished well ahead of the rest after 13 hard league encounters, registering 24 points to Garryowen's and Young Munster's 19 and fourth-placed St Mary's College's 18. Now it was a case of doing it all over again. On a weekend in Limerick, Shannon duly beat St Mary's, and the following day Garryowen beat Young Munster. The stage was set for the final at Lansdowne Road in Dublin, which it hardly need be said was attended by every dog-and-divil from totally rugby-mad Limerick.

Shannon won, and justice was served. Even if they had to rely on the place-kicking of wing Andrew Thompson, it was no indictment of their play; rather it was a tribute to Garryowen's spirited defence, which deprived the winners of a try. In this reporter's opinion, that 1998 All-Ireland triumph was the most efficient all round display of all Shannon's four title victories. Their forwards were, as usual, tough, hard, progressive and masterly at teamwork. The back row of Anthony Foley, Alan Quinlan and Eddie Halvey and lock Mick Galwey were particularly good.

But the Shannon backs are no longer mere aiders and abettors. Centre Rhys Ellison, a 31-year-old solicitor who has played for the New Zealand Maoris and had an All Black trial, was a particularly noteworthy contributor to Shannon's progress last season, as was Andrew Thompson, whose kicking earned him the Golden Boot award.

So it was Shannon, four times in a row and showing all the signs of getting better and better. And with the three Limerick clubs taking the first three places in the table, all the indications are that Limerick are set to dominate the All-Ireland League for the foreseeable future. Not, of course, that everything in the garden is rosy. The format for the first division of the AIB All-Ireland League is still a matter of some controversy. However, the Irish Rugby Union (IRFU) has decided to persist with the knockout competition for the top four finishers, and in this coming season of 1998-99 each division will also operate a two-up, two-down promotion and relegation system.

The basic IRFU policy is to concentrate on the three-tiered system of club, province and national team. Each province now has a professional manager, and the union has stipulated that each of the four provinces of Leinster, Ulster, Munster and Connacht will be subsidised by the IRFU for a semi-professional or full-time professional playing staff of up to 30 players each. Clubs are getting some financial help, mainly through prize money in the AIB League, but the emphasis is very much on the four branches.

If the national team suffered a 'whitewash' last season, the situation at all other levels of the Irish game was exceptionally good. Pride of place goes to the Under 19 team, which won the IRB/FIRA championship in Toulouse. They beat Argentina and South Africa before, remarkably, defeating France 18-0 in the final. The Under 21 side won the triple crown, beating England, Scotland and Wales, although they fell to France in La Roche, as did the Irish Universities. And the Irish Schools, so successful in recent times, lost only to England, at Stourbridge. The IRFU, at its annual meeting last June, remarked in its report, 'When one looks at these results, one can only be heartened by the quality and competitiveness of our under-age teams and a priority for the Union is to harness this talent and provide the support necessary to help these players maximise their potential.'

At national team level the priority is to entice the top players, so many of whom are contracted to English clubs, to return home and play for Irish clubs. Until recently the pleas tended to fall on deaf ears. The pull of the large salaries and the attraction of playing in such a highly publicised and highly competitive English league were too great. But there are signs that the situation is changing, or at least beginning to. Billy Lavery, a Belfast solicitor and chairman of the contracts sub-committee of the IRFU, has been quietly putting in place arrangements that many of the players are finding attractive. Some like Mark McCall, David Humphries, Justin Fitzpatrick and Gabriel Fulcher are definitely headed for home clubs, and the names of others have been mentioned. Whatever the merits and values of club and provincial competition, the IRFU is convinced that the basic foundation of the game is the international arena. It's the Test matches that are the financial bedrocks of rugby.

Ireland centre Mark McCall attacks Wasps for London Irish last season. McCall returns to Irish club rugby for 1998-99.

FRANCE – French turmoil

BY CHRIS THAU

If you believed English rugby was in a mess, spare a thought for the game in France, where the battle between the various factions is gathering momentum. Naturally, the object of the clash is money. A small group of clubs, nine in all, want a small professional competition with no more than 16 clubs. They argue that the size of the league is dictated by financial, sporting and promotional concerns. For all that, read money.

The leader of the nine, among them Bègles-Bordeaux, Brive, Castres, Toulouse and Agen, is Rene Bouscatel, a Toulouse lawyer. The leader of a second faction is the charismatic Serge Blanco, president of Biarritz Olympique, who passionately argues in favour of a 24-club competition. A third participant, although less vocal, is the French federation, led by its recently re-elected president, Bernard Lapasset. The fourth group, somewhere in the background, is the silent majority of French rugby, represented by the loquacious Monsieur Jacques Fouroux, the president of Auch rugby club and leader of the second division clubs. There is a fifth player, in the shape of Madame Marie-George Buffet, the French Sports Minister who got involved in the creation of the French Professional League and forced a new round of FFR elections.

Blanco is rightly recalling that the decision to have a 24-strong league, divided into two pools of 12, was unanimously taken by the presidents of the clubs at a meeting in March, and reconfirmed at the AGM of the Federation in June. He also pointed out that, personally, he has always favoured a smaller, 20-strong league, with two pools of 10, but that his proposal was rejected at the March meeting. The rest is simply a plot by the 'Big Nine' to get more money out of the communal pot, says the former French full back.

Former French full back Serge Blanco, now president of Biarritz Olympique, argues in favour of a 24-team French league.

Bouscatel, using legal jargon, argues a very obscure point about the size of the budget of the teams involved, claiming that 16, divided into two pools of 8, is in fact the optimal number of clubs in the French Professional League. His argument sounds familiar: TV money, clubs taken hostage by ERC, profit, investment etc. In a word, it is finance. Not unlike the English clubs, with whom they are in close contact, the Big Nine want to run their own affairs – a lucrative domestic league, followed by a European competition involving the English and the French clubs. All sides claim that they care for the future of French rugby and would like the French team to do well in the 1999 RWC.

The FFR supports the Blanco camp, due to his moderate position on the championship and Europe, and points out that a regional competition on the Super-12 model is the future and the saving grace of northern hemisphere rugby. With the two factions divided as ever, the Sports Ministry has been dragged into the dispute to act as a mediator. Jacques Fouroux, who paradoxically found himself on the same side of the barricade as Lapasset, criticised Bouscatel's stance, saying that it is the quality of the performance not the size of the budget that should give a club

Italy fly half Diego Dominguez, now calling the shots at Stade Français, the current French champions.

membership of the elite group. The National Olympic Committee (CNOSF) has been trying to find a compromise between the two warring sides, but without much success. While the ordinary supporter is trying to understand the intricacies of the argument, cynical observers argue that the apparent procrastination the Big Nine is in fact a smoke screen designed to cover their secret negotiations with the English clubs for the launch of a European professional league.

The vitriolic debate failed to cloud the end of a remarkable domestic season, which saw the spectacular re-emergence at the top of French rugby of Stade Français, more than a century after the club played in the first French Championship final. The club owner – or president – Max Guazziani managed to assemble a collection of ascending and fading stars under the charismatic management of former Bordeaux scrum half and coach Bernard Laporte.

Laporte brought with him to Paris three trusted foot-soldiers – the front-row trio Simon, Gimbert and Moscato, who served him well at Bordeaux when he captained the club to the French league title in 1991. With the implacable and more mature Moscato leading from the front, the three combined with a back row featuring Blond, Julliet, Pool-Jones, Moni and Marc Lievremont and an engine room selected from Roumat, Chaffardon, Auradou and Ross to secure a sizeable amount of raw material for Laporte's talented back division, led by the 'Little Prince' of Italian rugby, Diego Dominguez. Their combined talents helped Stade Français demolish Perpignan 34-7 in the final, but more significantly they managed to knock out the Rolls Royce of French rugby, Stade Toulousain, 39-3 in the semi-final, which made them hot favourites for the final played in the new Stade de France. The face of French rugby has changed beyond recognition.

Get a little extra help from the...

FIXTURES 1998–99

Note: English Allied Dunbar fixtures are provisional and may be subject to change.

AUGUST 1998

Sat, 29th	Welsh Premier Division
	Welsh League Division 1

SEPTEMBER 1998

Sat, 5th	Allied Dunbar Premiership 1, 2
	Jewson Nat Lges 1, 2N, 2S
	English Divisional League
	Tetley's Bitter Cup Prelim Rd
	Scottish Premiership
	Scottish National League
	Welsh Premier Division
	Welsh Lge 1, 2, 3W, 3E, 4W, 4E
Tue, 8th or	
Wed, 9th	Welsh Premier Division
Sat, 12th	Allied Dunbar Premiership 1, 2
	Jewson Nat Lges 1, 2N, 2S
	English Divisional League
	Scottish Premiership
	Scottish Nat Lge Divs 1-3
	Scottish Nat Cup 1st Round
	Welsh Premier Division
	Welsh Lge 1, 2, 3W, 3E, 4W, 4E
Sat, 19th	Allied Dunbar Premiership 1, 2
	Jewson Nat Lges Division 1
	Tetley's Bitter Cup 1st Round
	European Cup 1st Round
	Scottish Premiership
	Scottish National League
	Welsh Lge 1, 2, 3W, 3E, 4W, 4E
Tue, 22nd or	
Wed, 23rd	Welsh League Division 1
Sat, 26th	Allied Dunbar Premiership 1, 2
	Jewson Nat Lges 1, 2N, 2S
	English Divisional League
	European Cup 2nd Round
	Scottish Premiership
	Scottish National League
	SWALEC Cup 1st Round
	Welsh Lge 1, 2, 3W, 3E

OCTOBER 1998

Sat, 3rd	Allied Dunbar Premiership 1, 2
	Jewson Nat Lges 1, 2N, 2S
	English Divisional League
	Scottish Premiership
	Scottish National League
	Welsh Premier Division
	Welsh Lge 1, 2, 3W, 3E, 4W, 4E
Sat, 10th	Allied Dunbar Premiership 1, 2
	Jewson Nat Lges 1, 2N, 2S
	English Divisional League
	European Cup 3rd Round
	Scottish Premiership
	Scottish Nat Cup 2nd Round
	Welsh Lge 1, 2, 3W, 3E, 4W, 4E
Sat, 17th	Allied Dunbar Premiership 1, 2
	English Divisional League
	Tetley's Bitter Cup 2nd Round
	European Cup 4th Round
	Scottish Premiership
	Scottish National League
	Welsh Lge 1, 2, 3W, 3E, 4W, 4E
Sat, 24th	Allied Dunbar Premiership 1, 2
	Jewson Nat Lges 1, 2N, 2S
	English Divisional League
	Scottish Premiership
	Scottish National League
	Welsh Premier Division
	Welsh League Divisions 1, 2
	SWALEC Cup 2nd Round
Tue, 27th or	
Wed, 28th	Welsh League Division 1
Sat, 31st	Allied Dunbar Premiership 1, 2
	Jewson Nat Lges 1, 2N, 2S
	English Divisional League
	European Cup 5th Round
	Scottish Premiership
	Scottish National League
	Welsh Lge 2, 3W, 3E, 4W, 4E

NOVEMBER 1998

Wed, 4th	Netherlands v Barbarians (Amsterdam)
Sat, 7th	ITALY v ARGENTINA (TBA)
	Allied Dunbar Premiership 1, 2
	Jewson Nat Lges 1, 2N, 2S
	English Divisional League
	European Cup 6th Round
	Scottish Premiership
	Scottish National League
	Welsh Lge 1, 2, 3W, 3E, 4W, 4E
Tue, 10th or	
Wed, 11th	Glasgow & Caledonia v N Zealand Maoris (Scotland)
	Edinburgh & S Borders v South Africa (Scotland)
Wed, 11th	Combined Services v Barbarians (Portsmouth)
Sat, 14th	ENGLAND v NETHERLANDS (RWC Qual, Huddersfield)
	WALES v SOUTH AFRICA (Wembley)
	IRELAND v GEORGIA (RWC Qual, Dublin)

	Scotland v N Zealand Maoris (Murrayfield)
	Allied Dunbar Premiership 1
	Tetley's Bitter Cup 3rd Round
Sun, 15th	FRANCE v ARGENTINA (Nantes)
	Scottish Nat Cup 3rd Round
Tue, 17th or Wed, 18th	Glasgow & Caledonia v South Africa (Scotland)
	Edinburgh & S Borders v N Zealand Maoris (Scotland)
Wed, 18th	ITALY v NETHERLANDS (RWC Qual, Huddersfield)
	GEORGIA v ROMANIA (RWC Qual, Dublin)
Sat, 21st	FRANCE v AUSTRALIA (Paris)
	SCOTLAND v SOUTH AFRICA (Murrayfield)
	WALES v ARGENTINA (TBA)
	Allied Dunbar Premiership 1, 2
	Jewson Nat Lges 1, 2N, 2S
	English Divisional League
	Welsh Lge 1, 2, 3W, 3E, 4W, 4E
Sun, 22nd	ENGLAND v ITALY (RWC Qual, Huddersfield)
	IRELAND v ROMANIA (RWC Qual, Dublin)
	Glasgow & Caledonia v Canterbury (Scotland)
Sat, 28th	ENGLAND v AUSTRALIA (Twickenham)
	IRELAND v SOUTH AFRICA (Dublin)
	SCOTLAND v PORTUGAL (RWC Qual, Murrayfield)
	English League Cup 1st Round
	Jewson Nat Lges 1, 2N, 2S
	Welsh Premier Division
	Welsh League Division 1
	SWALEC Cup 3rd Round
Sun, 29th	Edinburgh & Scot Borders v Canterbury (Scotland)
	Scottish Nat Cup 4th Round

DECEMBER 1998

Tue, 1st or Wed, 2nd	PORTUGAL v SPAIN (RWC Qual, Scotland)
	Welsh Premier Division
Sat, 5th	ENGLAND v SOUTH AFRICA (Twickenham)
	SCOTLAND v SPAIN (RWC Qual, Murrayfield)
	English Lge Cup 2nd Round
	Jewson Nat Lges 1, 2N, 2S
	Welsh Premier Division

	Welsh Lge 1, 2, 3W, 3E, 4W, 4E
	AIB League Divisions 1-4
Sat, 5th to Sun, 6th	Dubai Sevens
Sun, 6th	Scottish Nat League Divs 4-7
Tue, 8th	Oxford v Cambridge U21s
	OXFORD v CAMBRIDGE (Twickenham)
Sat, 12th	Allied Dunbar Premiership 1, 2
	Jewson Nat Lges 1, 2N, 2S
	English Divisional League
	European Cup Quarter-finals
	Scottish Premiership
	Scottish National League
	Welsh Lge 1, 2, 3W, 3E, 4W, 4E
	AIB League Divisions 1-4
Sat, 19th	Allied Dunbar Premiership 1, 2
	Jewson Nat Lges 1, 2N, 2S
	English Divisional League
	Scottish Premiership
	Scottish National League
	SWALEC Cup 4th Round
	Welsh Lge 3W, 3E, 4W, 4E
	AIB League Divisions 1-4
Sun, 20th	Sunday's Well v Old Crescent (AIB 2, Cork)
*Sat, 26th	Allied Dunbar Premiership 1
	Jewson Nat Lges 1, 2N, 2S
	Welsh Premier Division
	Welsh League Division 1
	Dungannon v Malone (AIB 2, Dungannon)
	Old Wesley v Wanderers (AIB 2, Dublin)

*There will be selected Jewson Nat Leagues matches on Sun, 27th, and Mon, 28th.

JANUARY 1999

Sat, 2nd	Allied Dunbar Premiership 1, 2
	Jewson Nat Lges 1, 2N, 2S
	English Divisional League
	Welsh Premier Division
	Welsh Lge 1, 2, 3W, 3E, 4W, 4E
	AIB League Divisions 1-3
Sat, 9th	WALES v WESTERN SAMOA (Wales)
	Tetley's Bitter Cup 4th Round
	Jewson Nat Lges 2N, 2S
	English Divisional League
	European Cup Semi-finals
	Scottish Nat Cup 5th Round
	Welsh Lge 1, 2, 3W, 3E, 4W, 4E
	AIB League Divisions 1-4
Sun, 10th	Young Munster v Shannon (AIB 1, Cork)
	Old Wesley v Greystones (AIB 2, Dublin)
Sat, 16th	Allied Dunbar Premiership 1, 2
	Jewson Nat Lges 1, 2N, 2S

	English Divisional League
	Scottish Premiership
	Scottish National League
	Welsh Lge 1, 2, 3W, 3E, 4W, 4E
	AIB League Divisions 1-4
Sun, 17th	Corinthians v Bohemians
	(AIB 3, Galway)
Sat, 23rd	Allied Dunbar Premiership 1, 2
	Jewson Nat Lges 1, 2N, 2S
	English Divisional League
	Scottish Premiership
	Scottish National League
	Welsh Lge 2, 3W, 3E, 4W ,4E
	AIB League Divisions 1-4
	Bohemians v Dublin Univ
	(AIB 3, Munster)
Sat, 30th	European Cup Final
	Tetley's Bitter Cup 5th Round
	Jewson Nat Lges 1, 2N, 2S
	English Divisional League
	Scottish Premiership
	Scottish National League
	SWALEC Cup 5th Round
	Welsh Lge 1, 3W, 3E, 4W, 4E
	AIB Leagues Divisions 2-4

FEBRUARY 1999

Tue, 2nd or	
Wed, 3rd	Welsh League Division 1
Fri, 5th	Ireland U21 v France U21
	Ireland 'A' v France 'A'
	(both games in Ireland)
	Scotland U21 v Wales U21
	Scotland 'A' v Wales 'A'
	(both games in Edinburgh)
	Crawshay's Welsh v Scottish
	Cmbd Districts XV (Wales)
	IRELAND v FRANCE (Dublin)
Sat, 6th	Allied Dunbar Premiership 1, 2
	Jewson Nat Lges 1, 2N, 2S
	English Divisional League
Sat, 6th or	
Sun, 7th	SCOTLAND v WALES
	(Murrayfield)
Sat, 13th	Allied Dunbar Premiership 1, 2
	Jewson Nat Lges 1, 2N, 2S
	English Divisional League
	Scottish Cmbd Districts XV v
	Romania XV (Scotland)
	Scottish Nat Cup Quarter-finals
	Welsh Premier Division
	Welsh Lge 1, 2, 3W, 3E, 4W, 4E
	AIB League Divisions 1, 2 & 4
	Dublin Univ v UC Dublin
	(AIB 3, Dublin)
Fri, 19th	England U21 v Scotland U21
	England 'A' v Scotland 'A'
	(both games in N'hampton)
	Wales U21 v Ireland U21

	Wales 'A' v Ireland 'A'
	(both games in Wales)
Sat, 20th	ENGLAND v SCOTLAND
	(Calcutta Cup, Twickenham)
	English League Cup 3rd Round
Sat, 20th or	
Sun, 21st	WALES v IRELAND
	(Wembley)
Sat, 27th	Scottish Cmbd Districts XV v
	Spain (Scotland)
	Tetley's Bitter Cup Qtr-finals
	Allied Dunbar Premiership 2
	Jewson Nat Lges 1, 2N, 2S
	English Divisional League
	Scottish Premiership
	Scottish National League
	SWALEC Cup 6th Round
	Welsh Lge 2, 3W, 3E, 4W, 4E
	AIB League Divisions 1-4

MARCH 1999

Fri, 5th	France U21 v Wales U21
	France 'A' v Wales 'A'
	(both games in France)
	Ireland U21 v England U21
	Ireland 'A' v England 'A'
	(both games in Ireland)
	Italy U21 v Scotland U21
	Italy 'A' v Scotland 'A'
	(both in Treviso or Milan)
Sat, 6th	FRANCE v WALES (Paris)
	ITALY v SCOTLAND
	(Treviso or Milan)
	English League Cup 4th Round
Sat, 6th or	
Sun, 7th	IRELAND v ENGLAND
	(Dublin)
Sun, 7th	Scottish National League
Wed, 10th	East Midlands v Barbarians
	(Northampton)
Sat, 13th	Allied Dunbar Premiership 1, 2
	Jewson Nat Lges 1, 2N, 2S
	English Divisional League
	Scottish Cmbd Districts XV v
	Netherlands XV (Scotland)
	Scottish Premiership
	Scottish National League
	Welsh Premier Division
	Welsh Lge 1, 2, 3W, 3E, 4W, 4E
	AIB League Divisions 1, 2 & 4
Fri, 19th	England U21 v France U21
	(TBA)
	England 'A' v France 'A' (TBA)
	Scotland U21 v Ireland U21
	Scotland 'A' v Ireland 'A'
	(both games in Edinburgh)
	Leinster v Scottish Cmbd
	Districts XV (Ireland)

Sat, 20th   ENGLAND v FRANCE
                     (Twickenham)
                   ITALY v WALES
                     (Bologna)
                   English League Cup 5th Round
                   Welsh Lge 2, 4W, 4E
Sat, 20th or
Sun, 21st   SCOTLAND v IRELAND
                     (Murrayfield)
Tue, 23rd or
Wed, 24th   Welsh League Division 1
Wed, 24th   BUSA Finals
                     (Twickenham)
Wed, 24th to   IRB/FIRA World Youth
Sun, Apr 4th   Championships (Cardiff)
Fri, 26th to
Sun, 28th   Hong Kong Sevens
Sat, 27th   Allied Dunbar Premiership 1, 2
                   Jewson Nat Lges 1, 2N, 2S
                   English Divisional League
                   Daily Mail Schools Day
                     (Twickenham)
                   Scottish Premiership
                   Scottish National League
                   SWALEC Cup Quarter-finals
                   Welsh Lge 1, 2, 3W, 3E, 4W, 4E
                   AIB League Divisions 1 & 2
Wed, 31st   Army v RAF (Aldershot)
Note: Leicester v Barbarians is scheduled for
March 1999; date to be confirmed.

APRIL 1999
Sat, 3rd   Tetley's Bitter Cup Semi-finals
                   Allied Dunbar Premiership 2
                   Jewson Nat Lges 1, 2N, 2S
                   Scottish Nat Cup Semi-finals
                   Welsh Premier Division
                   Welsh Lge 1, 2, 3W, 3E, 4W, 4E
                   AIB League Divisions 2 & 4
Fri, 9th   France U21 v Scotland U21
                     (Brive)
                   France 'A' v Scotland 'A'
                     (Toulouse)
                   Wales U21 v England U21
                   Wales 'A' v England 'A'
                     (both games in Wales)
Sat, 10th &
Sun, 11th   AIB League Division 2
Sat, 10th   FRANCE v SCOTLAND
                     (Paris)
                   English League Cup 6th Round
Sun, 11th   WALES v ENGLAND
                     (Wembley)
Wed, 14th   RAF v RN (Gloucester)
Sat, 17th   Allied Dunbar Premiership 1, 2
                   Jewson Nat Lges 1, 2N, 2S
                   Tetley's Bitter Vase Final
                     (Twickenham)

NPI Cup Final
  (Twickenham)
English Divisional League
SWALEC Cup Semi-finals
Welsh Lge 1, 2, 3W, 3E, 4W, 4E
AIB League Division 2
Tue, 20th or
Wed, 21st   Welsh Premier Div Phase II
Sat 24th   RN v Army (Twickenham)
                   Allied Dunbar Premiership 1, 2
                   Welsh Premier Div Phase II
                   Welsh Lge 1, 2, 3W, 3E, 4W, 4E
Tue, 27th or
Wed, 28th   Welsh Premier Div Phase II

MAY 1999
Sat, 1st   Allied Dunbar Premiership 1, 2
                   Welsh Premier Div Phase II
                   Welsh Lge 1, 2, 3W, 3E, 4W, 4E
Tue, 3rd or
Wed, 4th   Welsh Premier Div Phase II
Sat, 8th   Allied Dunbar Premiership 1, 2
                   Scottish National Cup Finals
                     (Murrayfield)
                   Welsh Premier Division Final
                     Phase II Matches
Wed, 12th   Allied Dunbar Premiership
                     Play-offs
Sat, 15th   Tetley's Bitter Cup Final
                     (Twickenham)
                   SWALEC Cup Final (TBA)
Sun, 16th   Allied Dunbar Premiership
                     Play-offs
Sat, 22nd   Tetley's Bitter C'ty Ch'ships
(prov)   Finals (Twickenham)
Sun, 23rd   Sanyo Cup
(prov)   (Twickenham)
Sat, 29th   Middlesex Charity 7s Finals
(prov)   (Twickenham)
Note: ROMANIA and IRELAND are scheduled
to meet in Bucharest in May 1999; date to be
confirmed.

OCTOBER 1999
Fri, 1st   RWC pool matches begin
Wed, 20th   RWC Quarter-finals play-offs
                     (Twickenham, Murrayfield)
Sat, 23rd   RWC Quarter-final (Cardiff)
Sun, 24th   RWC Quarter-final (Paris)
                   RWC Quarter-final
                     (Murrayfield)
                   RWC Quarter-final (Dublin)
Sat, 30th   RWC Semi-final (Twickenham)
Sun, 31st   RWC Semi-final (Twickenham)

NOVEMBER 1999
Thur, 4th   RWC Third-place Match
                     (Cardiff)
Sat, 6th   RWC Final (Cardiff)

performance from

N E X T

REVIEW OF THE
SEASON 1997-98

A SUMMARY OF THE SEASON 1997-98

BY BILL MITCHELL

INTERNATIONAL RUGBY

ARGENTINA IN NEW ZEALAND
JUNE & JULY 1997

Opponents		Results
New Zealand Maoris	L	17-39
Nelson-Bays-Marlborough	W	42-10
NEW ZEALAND	L	8-93
Taranaki	L	10-26
NEW ZEALAND	L	10-62

Played 5 Won 1 Lost 4

ROMANIA IN WALES
AUGUST 1997

Opponents		Results
Wales 'A'	L	21-36
WALES	L	21-70

Played 2 Lost 2

AUSTRALIA IN ARGENTINA & EUROPE
OCTOBER & NOVEMBER 1997

Opponents		Results
Tucuman	W	76-15
Rosario	W	29-18
ARGENTINA	W	23-15
Buenos Aires XV	W	17-12
ARGENTINA	L	16-18
ENGLAND	D	15-15
SCOTLAND	W	37- 8

Played 7 Won 5 Drawn 1 Lost 1

TONGA IN ENGLAND, SCOTLAND & WALES
OCTOBER & NOVEMBER 1997

Opponents		Results
Redruth President's XV	W	64- 9
Bristol	L	15-35
Edinburgh	L	14-26
Oxford University	W	31-16
Bridgend	W	21-18
Bath	W	29-13
WALES	L	12-46
Sale	W	26-14
Leeds	L	15-29
Saracens	L	8-83

Played 10 Won 5 Lost 5

NEW SOUTH WALES IN ENGLAND,
SCOTLAND & WALES
NOVEMBER 1997

Opponents		Results
Border Reivers	W	69-20
London Irish	W	52- 7
Richmond	L	24-43
Cardiff	W	34-30

Played 4 Won 3 Lost 1

NEW ZEALAND IN BRITISH ISLES
NOVEMBER & DECEMBER 1997

Opponents		Results
Llanelli	W	81- 3
Wales 'A'	W	51- 8
IRELAND	W	63-15
Emerging England	W	59-22
ENGLAND	W	25- 8
Allied Dunbar Select	W	18-11
WALES	W	42- 7
England 'A'	W	30-19
ENGLAND	D	26-26

Played 9 Won 8 Drawn 1

SOUTH AFRICA IN EUROPE
NOVEMBER & DECEMBER 1997

Opponents		Results
ITALY	W	62-31
French Barbarians	L	22-40
FRANCE	W	36-32
France 'A'	L	7-21
FRANCE	W	52-10
ENGLAND	W	29-11
SCOTLAND	W	68-10

Played 7 Won 5 Lost 2

AUSTRALIAN CAPITAL TERRITORY IN
ENGLAND & SCOTLAND
NOVEMBER & DECEMBER 1997

Opponents		Results
Moseley	W	46-26
Cambridge University	L	27-36
Scottish Borders	W	26-15
Dean Richards XV	W	64-45

Bath	W	20-13
Caledonia	W	36-20
Glasgow	W	22- 6

Played 7 Won 6 Lost 1

CANADA IN IRELAND
NOVEMBER 1997

Opponents	Results	
Ireland 'A'	L	10-26
IRELAND	L	11-33

Played 2 Lost 2

NORTHERN TRANSVAAL BULLS
IN WALES & SCOTLAND
NOVEMBER & DECEMBER 1997

Opponents	Results	
Swansea	D	34-34
Pontypridd	L	0-18
Llanelli	L	21-27
Scotland 'A'	W	31-15

Played 4 Won 1 Drawn 1 Lost 2

GAUTENG FALCONS IN ENGLAND & WALES
JANUARY & FEBRUARY 1998

Opponents	Results	
Bedford	L	17-31
Harlequins	L	21-31
Pontypridd	W	40-32

Played 3 Won 1 Lost 2

SCOTLAND IN FIJI & AUSTRALIA
MAY & JUNE 1998

Opponents	Results	
FIJI	L	26-51
Victoria	W	42-13
New S'th Wales Country	W	34-13
New South Wales	W	34-10
Australian Barbarians	L	34-39
AUSTRALIA	L	3-45
Queensland	L	22-27
AUSTRALIA	L	11-33

Played 8 Won 3 Lost 5

IRELAND IN SOUTH AFRICA
MAY & JUNE 1998

Opponents	Results	
Boland	W	48-25
South West Districts	L	20-27
Western Province	L	6-12
Griqualand West	L	13-52
SOUTH AFRICA	L	13-37
North West Districts	W	26-18
SOUTH AFRICA	L	0-33

Played 7 Won 2 Lost 5

ENGLAND IN AUSTRALIA, NEW ZEALAND &
SOUTH AFRICA
JUNE & JULY 1998

Opponents	Results	
AUSTRALIA	L	0-76
New Zealand 'A'	L	10-18
New Zealand Academy	L	32-50
NEW ZEALAND	L	22-64
New Zealand Maoris	L	14-62
NEW ZEALAND	L	10-40
SOUTH AFRICA		

Played 7 Lost 7

WALES IN ZIMBABWE & SOUTH AFRICA
JUNE 1998

Opponents	Results	
ZIMBABWE	W	49-11
Emerging Springboks	L	13-35
Border	L	8-24
Natal	L	23-30
Gauteng Falcons	L	37-39
SOUTH AFRICA	L	13-96

Played 6 Won 1 Lost 5

FRANCE IN ARGENTINA & FIJI
JUNE 1998

Opponents	Results	
ARGENTINA	W	35-18
Buenos Aires XV	L	22-36
ARGENTINA	W	37-12
Fiji Warriors	W	36-32
FIJI	W	34- 9

Played 5 Won 4 Lost 1

TONGA IN NEW ZEALAND
JUNE 1998

Opponents	Results	
Counties-Manakau	W	22-15
Thames Valley	W	24-10
New Zealand Maoris	L	7-66
Wanganui	W	27-20
New Zealand Academy	L	0-48
New Zealand 'A'	L	7-60

Played 6 Won 3 Lost 3

THE FIVE NATIONS
CHAMPIONSHIP 1998

Results			
France	24	England	17
Ireland	16	Scotland	17
England	60	Wales	26
Scotland	16	France	51
France	18	Ireland	16
Wales	19	Scotland	13

Sanyo digiCAM.
Kicks photography into touch.

Capture up to 120 shots of the action with no film and no fuss.

The new Sanyo digiCAM introduces digital Video Clip technology allowing you to capture four 5 second bursts of key action sequences with sound.

Save your clip to its 4MB SmartMedia card and download to your PC, Mac or view through your television and save onto VHS cassette tape.

Images you can e-mail or display within business presentations or simply keep to relive that great moment.

Your imagination and digiCAM advance performance technology. Always a winning combination.

SANYO | digiCAM

WHAT THE WORLD'S COMING TO

Ireland	21	Wales	30
Scotland	20	England	34
England	35	Ireland	17
Wales	0	France	51

	P	W	L	F	A	Pts
France	4	4	0	144	49	8
England	4	3	1	146	87	6
Wales	4	2	2	75	145	4
Scotland	4	1	3	66	120	2
Ireland	4	0	4	70	100	0

TRI-NATIONS TOURNAMENT

Australia*	24	New Zealand	16
Australia	13	South Africa	14
New Zealand	3	South Africa	13
New Zealand*	23	Australia	27
South Africa	24	New Zealand	23
South Africa	29	Australia	15

	P	W	D	L	F	A	Pts
South Africa	4	4	0	0	80	54	17
Australia	4	2	0	2	79	82	10
New Zealand	4	0	0	4	65	88	2

* Bledisloe Cup matches
Additional Bledisloe Cup match:

Australia	19	New Zealand	14

OTHER INTERNATIONAL MATCHES 1997-98

FULL INTERNATIONAL RESULTS

Latin Cup

France	30	Italy	19
Argentina	45	Romania	18
Argentina	18	Italy	18
France	39	Romania	3
France	32	Argentina	27
Italy	35	Romania	32

	P	W	D	L	F	A	Pts
France	3	3	0	0	101	49	9
Argentina	3	1	1	1	90	68	6
Italy	3	1	1	1	92	80	6
Romania	3	0	0	3	53	139	3

Italy	33	Ireland	18
Italy	25	Scotland	21
Wales	23	Italy	20

Pacific Rim Championship

Japan	23	Canada	30
Hong Kong	23	Canada	17
Hong Kong	43	USA	25
USA	38	Japan	27
Hong Kong	31	Japan	38
Canada	17	USA	15
USA	3	Canada	37
Japan	16	Hong Kong	17
USA	21	Japan	25
Canada	38	Hong Kong	12
Canada	34	Japan	24
Hong Kong	27	USA	17

	P	W	L	F	A	Bon	Pts
Canada	6	5	1	173	99	2	22
Hong Kong	6	4	2	156	151	1	17
Japan	6	2	4	152	171	4	12
USA	6	1	5	119	179	4	8

'A' INTERNATIONAL RESULTS

France	32	England	17
Ireland	9	Scotland	11
England	22	Wales	41
Scotland	24	France	20
France	30	Ireland	30
Scotland	44	England	14
England	40	Ireland	30
Wales	18	France	27
Wales	10	Scotland	18
Ireland	27	Wales	42

	P	W	D	L	F	A	Pts
Scotland	4	4	0	0	97	53	8
France	4	2	1	1	75	50	5
Wales	4	2	0	2	111	94	4
England	4	1	0	3	93	147	2
Ireland	4	0	1	3	96	123	1

UNDER 21 INTERNATIONAL RESULTS

France	15	England	16
Ireland	23	Scotland	7
England	46	Wales	7
Scotland	9	France	22
France	35	Ireland	11
Wales	3	Scotland	10
Ireland	27	Wales	25
Scotland	16	England	32
England	7	Ireland	9
Wales	13	France	3

	P	W	D	L	F	A	Pts
England	4	3	0	1	101	47	6
Ireland	4	3	0	1	70	74	6
France	4	2	0	2	75	49	4
Wales	4	1	0	3	48	86	2
Scotland	4	1	0	3	42	80	2

Italy	15	Scotland	41
England	42	France	27

STUDENT AND UNIVERSITY MATCHES 1997-98

France Studs	34	England Studs	20
France Studs	64	England Studs	16
England Studs	24	Wales Studs	15
Wales Studs	6	France Studs	15
Irish Univs	25	Scottish Univs	11
English Univs	15	Welsh Univs	24
*Welsh Univs	7	Scottish Univs	0
Irish Univs	44	Welsh Univs	24
Scottish Univs	46	English Univs	10
English Univs	30	Irish Univs	80

*Match abandoned owing to Scottish injury.

SCHOOLS 18 GROUP MATCHES 1997-98

Scotland	3	France	20
Wales	54	Scotland	0
Wales	28	France	25
Scotland	5	England	56
England	11	Wales	10
Ireland	49	Scotland	0
France	22	England	8
Ireland	13	Wales	6
England	26	Ireland	22

	P	W	L	F	A	Pts	%
England	4	3	1	101	59	7	75
Ireland	3	2	1	84	32	4	66
France	3	2	1	67	32	4	66
Wales	4	2	2	98	49	4	50
Scotland	4	0	4	8	179	0	0

YOUTH (UNDER 19) MATCHES 1997-98

Scotland	39	Canada	19
England	41	Scotland	0
England	10	Argentina	3
Wales	20	England	29

COLTS (UNDER 18) MATCHES 1997-98

Ireland	14	Italy	11
Portugal	6	Wales	19
Wales	29	Romania	13
Ireland	26	Italy	19
Wales	0	Ireland	15
France	15	Wales	6
Ireland	63	Spain	0
Scotland	18	Spain	7
Wales	23	Italy	14
Scotland	34	Romania	14
Wales	0	Ireland	15
England	41	Scotland	0
Wales	20	England	29
Scotland	10	Wales	11
England	17	France	18
Ireland	25	Scotland	14
Scotland	11	Wales	13

JUNIOR WORLD CUP (HELD IN FRANCE)

Preliminary and classification matches

Ireland	47	USA	13
Scotland	3	Chile	7
Wales	19	Canada	23
Ireland	17	South Africa	17

(South Africa won a penalty 'shoot-out' but were then disqualified for using an illegal kicker.)

Wales	20	Scotland	7
Scotland	56	Spain	10
Wales	39	Japan	10
Scotland	45	Russia	5
Wales	34	Romania	19

Semi-finals

Ireland	18	Argentina	3
France	53	Canada	6

Final

France	0	Ireland	18

HONG KONG SEVENS

Cup Final

Fiji	28	Western Samoa	19

Plate Final

Korea	49	Papua NG	14

Bowl Final

Morocco	31	Taiwan	14

OTHER MAJOR SEVENS FINALS

Dubai:

New Zealand	24	Fiji	21

Buenos Aires:

Argentina	19	New Zealand	40

WOMEN'S WORLD CUP (HELD IN HOLLAND)

Quarter-finals

USA	25	Scotland	10
Canada	9	France	7
England	30	Australia	13
New Zealand	46	Spain	3

Semi-finals

New Zealand	44	England	11
USA	46	Canada	6

Final

New Zealand	44	USA	12

Third-place Play-off

England	81	Canada	15

Plate Final

Australia	25	Scotland	15

WOMEN'S FOUR NATIONS CHAMPIONSHIP 1997-98

Results

England	29	Wales	12
Ireland	0	Scotland	15
Wales	15	Scotland	27
Scotland	8	England	5
Ireland	10	Wales	27
England	62	Ireland	8

	P	W	D	L	F	A	Pts
Scotland	3	3	0	0	50	17	8
England	3	2	0	1	96	28	6
Wales	3	1	0	2	51	66	2
Ireland	3	0	0	3	18	104	0

OTHER WOMEN'S INTERNATIONAL MATCHES 1997-98

New Zealand	67	England	0
France	5	England	13
France 'A'	8	England 'A'	27
Wales Select	5	Emerging England	27
Emerging England	12	Ireland 'A'	0

CLUB, COUNTY AND DIVISIONAL RUGBY

ENGLAND

Tetley's Bitter Cup
Quarter-finals

London Irish	7	Wasps	41
Northampton	17	Newcastle	7
Richmond	30	Saracens	36
West Hartlepool	21	Sale	36

Semi-finals

Northampton	10	Saracens	25
Wasps	15	Sale	9

Final

Saracens	48	Wasps	18

Tetley's Bitter Vase Final
Huddersfield
YMCA 40   West Leeds   8

NPI Pensions Cup Final
Bedford Athletic   29   Stroud   24
(after extra time)

Allied Dunbar Premiership
Premier One

	P	W	D	L	F	A	Pts
Newcastle	22	19	0	3	645	387	38
Saracens	22	18	1	3	584	396	37
Bath	22	13	0	9	575	455	26
Leicester	22	12	2	8	569	449	26
Richmond	22	12	0	10	607	499	24
Gloucester	22	11	1	10	512	528	23
Sale	22	10	2	10	605	558	22
N'ton	22	9	1	12	493	472	19
Wasps	22	8	1	13	490	609	17
Harlequins	22	8	0	14	516	645	16
London I	22	6	0	16	457	673	12
Bristol	22	2	0	20	351	733	4

Relegated: Bristol

Premier Two

	P	W	D	L	F	A	Pts
Bedford	22	20	0	2	791	365	40
W H'pool	22	15	1	6	617	431	31
L Scottish	22	14	1	7	517	404	29
Rotherham	22	14	0	8	566	386	28
Orrell	22	12	0	10	533	400	24
Moseley	22	11	1	10	478	421	23
Coventry	22	11	1	10	444	532	23
Waterloo	22	11	0	11	510	525	22
Blackheath	22	8	0	14	474	621	16
Wakefield	22	6	0	16	382	556	12
Exeter	22	6	0	16	334	553	12
Fylde	22	2	0	20	258	710	4

Promoted: Bedford, W H'pool, L Scottish
Relegated: None

Jewson National League
1st Division champions: Worcester
Runners-up: Leeds
2nd Division North champions:
Birmingham Solihull
Runners-up: Manchester
2nd Division South champions: Camberley
Runners-up: Henley

Tetley's Bitter County Championship
Semi-finals

Cornwall	21	Gloucestershire	9
Yorkshire	21	Cheshire	33

Final

Cheshire	21	Cornwall	14

Tetley's Bitter U21 County Championship
Final

Cumbria	7	East Midlands	31

University Match
Oxford U   17   Cambridge U   29
University Second Teams Match
Oxford U   27   Cambridge U   19
University U21 Match
Oxford U   19   Cambridge U   18
Women's University Match
Oxford U   22   Cambridge U   5

British Universities Final
Swansea U   17   Northumbria U   3
British Universities Women's Final
Edinburgh U   19   Cardiff U   17

Sanyo Cup
Newcastle   47   World XV   41

Cheltenham & Gloucester Cup Final
Bedford   25   Gloucester   33

Inter-Services Champions: The Army

Middlesex 7s Winners: Barbarians
London (Rosslyn Park) 7s Winners:
Cambridge U
Shell UK Ltd-Rosslyn Park Schools Sevens
Festival Winners: Cheltenham
Open Winners: John Fisher
Colts Winners: Brighton
Junior Winners: Whitgift
Preparatory School Winners: Millfield
Girls' Schools Winners: John Cleveland

Bread for Life Women's National Cup Final
Saracens   5   Wasps   0
Women's National Champions: Saracens
Women's National 7s Winners: Saracens

ALWAYS ONE TO SPOT A GOOD OPENING, ONCE ARCHIE HEARD ABOUT SAVE & PROSPER UNIT TRUSTS, THERE WAS NO STOPPING HIM

If you'd like to hear more about Save & Prosper Unit Trusts, just ring us on our free Moneyline: 0800 829 100. It could be just the break you need.

SAVE & PROSPER

WALES

SWALEC Welsh Challenge Cup
Quarter-finals

Ebbw Vale	27	Swansea	13
Llanelli	40	Neath	17
Newport	29	Pontypridd	27
Seven Sisters	39	Garndiffaith	0

Semi-finals

Ebbw Vale	44	Newport	10
Llanelli	61	Seven Sisters	16

Final

Llanelli	19	Ebbw Vale	12

Welsh Challenge Trophy Final

Pontypridd	15	Cardiff	10

National Leagues
Premier Division

	P	W	D	L	T	B	Pts
Swansea	14	11	2	1	68	11	46
Cardiff	14	10	1	3	59	9	40
Pontypridd	14	8	2	4	55	9	35
Ebbw Vale	14	8	0	6	33	3	27
Neath	14	6	1	7	41	4	23
Llanelli	14	5	2	7	44	5	22
Bridgend	14	3	2	9	33	1	12
Newport	14	0	0	14	23	2	0**

Relegated: Bridgend, Newport
**Denotes points deducted

First Division

	P	W	D	L	T	B	Pts
Caerphilly	30	27	0	3	137	18	99
Aberavon	30	20	2	8	104	12	74
Treorchy	30	19	0	11	115	16	73
Bonymaen	30	17	0	13	86	9	60
Dunvant	30	17	1	12	87	6	58
Merthyr	30	14	4	12	91	8	54
Llandovery	30	14	0	16	88	12	54
Rumney	30	15	1	14	94	7	53
Newbridge	30	14	0	16	61	8	50
Cross Keys	30	14	1	15	79	6	49
Abertillery	30	14	1	15	64	4	47
S Wales Police	30	10	1	19	93	11	42
Pontypool	30	12	1	17	73	3	40
Blackwood	30	12	0	18	72	4	40
UWIC (Card. In.)	30	8	0	22	87	11	35
Maesteg	30	7	0	23	59	2	23

Promoted: Caerphilly, Aberavon
Relegated: UWIC (Cardiff Institute), Maesteg

2nd Division champions: Tredegar
Runners-up: Tondu
3rd Division champions: Llantrisant
Runners-up: Rhymney
4th Division champions: Vardre
Runners-up: Gilfach Goch

SCOTLAND

Tennnents Inter-District Championship

	P	W	D	L	F	A	Pts
Edinburgh	3	2	0	1	76	55	4
Glasgow	3	2	0	1	67	49	4
Caledonia	3	2	0	1	49	54	4
Scot. Borders	3	0	0	3	34	68	0

SRU Tennents Velvet Cup Final

Glasgow Hawks	36	Kelso	14

SRU Tennents Velvet Shield Final

Selkirk	17	Berwick	11

SRU Tennents Velvet Bowl Final

Perthshire	10	Carnoustie HS FP	8

SRU League Trophy Final

Edinburgh Ac	37	Stirling County	41

Scottish 7s Winners:
Kelso: Kelso
Selkirk: Kelso
Gala: Glasgow Hawks
Melrose: Melrose
Hawick: Hawick
Earlston: Kelso
Langholm: Gala
Jed-Forest: Kelso
**Radio Borders/
Borders Toyota Kings of Sevens:** Kelso

SRU Tennents Premiership
First Division A

	P	W	L	F	A	B	Pts
Watsonians	13	9	4	397	201	8	44
Melrose	13	9	4	331	230	7	43
W of Scotland	13	8	5	301	233	7	39
Currie	13	7	6	260	335	4	32
Hawick	13	6	7	262	259	2	26

First Division B

	P	W	L	F	A	B	Pts
Boroughmuir	13	8	5	318	213	5	37
Stirling County	13	6	7	208	236	3	27
Jed-Forest	13	5	8	219	388	2	22
Heriot's FP	13	5	8	255	302	1	21
Edinburgh Ac	13	2	11	209	353	5	13

1st Division champions: Watsonians
2nd Division A winners: Glasgow Hawks
2nd Division B winners: Kirkcaldy
2nd Division champions: Glasgow Hawks
3rd Division A winners: Selkirk
3rd Division B winners: Glenrothes
3rd Division champions: Selkirk

IRELAND

Inter-Provincial Championship

	P	W	D	L	F	A	Pts
Leinster	3	2	0	1	61	46	4
Munster	3	2	0	1	56	43	4
Ulster	3	1	0	2	64	65	2
Connacht	3	1	0	2	42	69	2

Senior Provincial Cup Winners:
Connacht: Corinthians
Leinster: Lansdowne
Munster: Shannon
Ulster: Dungannon

AIB All-Ireland League
Division 1

	P	W	D	L	F	A	Pts
Shannon	13	12	0	1	367	142	24
Garryowen	13	9	1	3	360	224	19
Young Munster	13	9	1	3	244	176	19
St Mary's Coll	13	9	0	4	409	274	18
Cork Const	13	8	0	5	289	217	16
Ballymena	13	7	0	6	344	287	14
Clontarf	13	7	0	6	276	266	14
Terenure Coll	13	5	1	7	241	262	11
Lansdowne	13	4	2	7	264	328	10
Blackrock Coll	13	4	1	8	249	326	9
Dungannon	13	4	0	9	239	309	8
Dolphin	13	3	2	8	227	345	8
Old Crescent	13	4	0	9	168	298	8
Old Belvedere	13	2	0	11	208	431	4

Division 2

	P	W	D	L	F	A	Pts
Galwegians	13	13	0	0	336	164	26
Buccaneers §§	12	11	0	1	311	102	22
Sunday's Well	13	7	2	4	254	227	16
City of Derry	13	8	0	5	277	255	16
Univ Coll Cork	13	6	1	6	204	282	13
Skerries	13	6	0	7	248	224	12
De la S'e-P'ston	13	6	0	7	280	269	12
Old Wesley	13	5	1	7	256	248	12
Greystones	13	5	1	7	204	211	11
Bective Rangers	13	5	1	7	210	233	11
Malone	13	5	0	8	210	255	10
Wanderers §§	12	5	0	7	200	254	10
Monkstown	13	3	0	10	207	336	6
Instonians	13	2	0	11	205	341	4

§§Outstanding match not played.

Division 3 champions: Portadown
Runners-up: Ballynahinch
Division 4 champions: County Carlow
Runners-up: Richmond

FRANCE

French Club Championship
Semi-finals

Stade Fr-CASG	39	Toulouse	3
Colomiers	13	Perpignan	15

Final

Stade Fr-CASG	34	Perpignan	7

French Cup Final

Toulouse	22	Stade Fr-CASG	15

ITALY

Italian Cup
Semi-finals (aggregate scores)

Treviso	63	Roma	36
Padova	43	Rovigo	25

Final

Treviso	9	Padova	3

NEW ZEALAND

Championship First Division 1997
Semi-finals

Auckland	15	Canterbury	21
Waikato	40	C'ties-Manakau	43

Final

Canterbury	44	C'ties-Manakau	13

Ranfurly Shield Holders: Canterbury

SOUTH AFRICA

Currie Cup 1997
Semi-finals

Natal	22	Free State	40
W Province	38	Gauteng Lions	18

Final

W Province	14	Free State	12

BARBARIAN FC

Opponents	Results	
Combined Services	W	40-23
East Midlands	W	50-40
Leicester	W	73-19

Played 3 Won 3

SUPER-12 TOURNAMENT

Final Table

	P	W	D	L	F	A	Pts
Auckland Blues	11	9	0	2	388	298	43
Cant. Crusaders	11	8	0	3	340	260	41
Coastal Sharks	11	7	0	4	329	263	36
Otago H'landers	11	7	0	4	343	279	34
Q'land Reds	11	6	1	4	273	229	31
NSW Waratahs	11	6	1	4	306	276	30
Chiefs	11	6	0	5	279	291	29
Hurricanes	11	5	0	6	313	342	26
W'n Stormers	11	3	0	8	248	364	18
ACT Brumbies	11	3	0	8	228	308	17
Northern Bulls	11	3	0	8	249	306	16
Golden Cats	11	2	0	9	266	345	15

Semi-finals

Auckland Blues	37	Otago H'landers	31
Cant. Crusaders	36	Coastal Sharks	32

Final

Cant. Crusaders	20	Auckland Blues	13

Mission Statement

The Wooden Spoon Society aims to enhance the quality
and prospect of life for children and young persons in the
United Kingdom who are presently disadvantaged either
physically, mentally or socially

Charity Registration No: 326691